Instructor's Manual

with Test Bank for

Understanding Statistics in the Behavioral Sciences

Sixth Edition

Robert R. Pagano
University of Pittsburgh

WADSWORTH
THOMSON LEARNING™
Australia • Canada • Mexico • Singapore • Spain • United Kingdom • United States

Printed in the United States of America

1 2 3 4 5 6 7 04 03 02 01 00

ISBN 0-534-57773-3

For more information, contact
Wadsworth/Thomson Learning
10 Davis Drive
Belmont, CA 94002-3098
USA

For more information about our products, contact us:
Thomson Learning Academic Resource Center
1-800-423-0563
http://www.wadsworth.com

International Headquarters
Thomson Learning
International Division
290 Harbor Drive, 2nd Floor
Stamford, CT 06902-7477
USA

UK/Europe/Middle East/South Africa
Thomson Learning
Berkshire House
168-173 High Holborn
London WC1V 7AA
United Kingdom

Asia
Thomson Learning
60 Albert Complex, #15-01
Singapore 189969

Canada
Nelson Thomson Learning
1120 Birchmount Road
Toronto, Ontario M1K 5G4
Canada

TABLE OF CONTENTS

PART I TEST ITEMS

PART II ADDENDUM

PREFACE

TO THE INSTRUCTOR

I have been teaching a course in introductory statistics for over 30 years, first within the Department of Psychology at the University of Washington and most recently within the Department of Neuroscience at the University of Pittsburgh. This textbook is the mainstay of the course. Most of my students have been psychology majors, but many have also come from biology, business, education, neuroscience, nursing, and other fields. Because most of these students do not have high aptitude for mathematics and are not well grounded in mathematical skills, I have used an informal rather than strictly mathematical approach. This approach assumes only high school algebra for background knowledge. It relies on clarity of presentation, a particularly effective sequencing of the inferential material, detailed verbal description, interesting illustrative examples, and many fully solved practice problems to help students understand the material.

My statistics course has been quite successful. Students are able to grasp the material, even the more complicated topics such as "power," and at the same time many even enjoy learning it. Student ratings of this course have been quite high. They rate the textbook even higher, saying among other things that it is very clear; they like the touches of humor; and that it helps to have the material presented in such great detail.

In preparing the sixth edition, I have been guided again by advice and feedback from students and professors. I am very pleased that this feedback has been quite positive and that for most of the textbook the advice has been not to change anything because the text works very well. However, there are three recommended major changes that I have made in the sixth edition. First, the chapter on power that had been removed in the fifth edition has been put back into the sixth edition; it is Chapter 11. Second, I have eliminated the separate chapter on the Mann-Whitney *U* test. Instead, the material on the Mann-Whitney *U* test (Chapter 12 in the fifth edition) has been condensed and included with the other nonparametric tests in Chapter 18. Finally, due to the recent recognition of the importance of "Size of Effect", I have introduced this topic in Chapter 11 of the sixth edition with a general discussion of it in conjunction with power, and shown how to compute the size of effect in conjunction with the "t Test for Independent Groups" in Chapter 14, and with "One-Way Analysis of Variance" in Chapter 15.

Textbook Rationale

This is an introductory textbook that covers both descriptive and inferential statistics. It is intended for students majoring in the behavioral sciences. For many of these students, statistics is a subject that elicits considerable anxiety and which is avoided as long as possible. Moreover, I think it is fair to say that when the usual undergraduate course is completed, many students have not understood much of the inferential statistics material. This is partly because the material is inherently difficult and the students themselves are not proficient in mathematics. However, in my opinion, this situation also exists because most textbooks do a poor job of explaining inferential statistics to this group of students. These texts usually err in one or more of the following ways: (1) they are not clearly written; (2) they are not sufficiently detailed; (3) they present the material too mathematically; (4) they present the material at too low a level; (5) they do not give a sufficient number of fully solved problems for the student to practice on; and (6) in inferential statistics, they use an inappropriate sequence of topics, beginning with the sampling distribution of the mean.

In this and the previous five editions, I have tried to correct such deficiencies through an informal writing style; a clearly written, detailed, and theoretically oriented presentation that requires only high school algebra for understanding; the inclusion of many interesting, fully solved practice problems that are located immediately following the relevant expository material; and a better sequencing of the inferential material.

I believe a key to understanding inferential statistics is the material presented in the beginning inferential chapters and its sequencing. In my opinion, optimal learning of the material occurs by using the sign test as the first inference test encountered by the student and by using the following sequence of topics: random sampling and probability, binomial distribution, introduction to hypothesis testing using the sign test, power, sampling distributions (including their empirical generation), sampling distribution of the mean, z test for single samples, t test for single samples, confidence intervals, t test for correlated and independent groups, introduction to analysis of variance, multiple comparisons, two-way ANOVA, nonparametric tests, and finally, a review of all of inferential statistics.

At the heart of statistical inference lies the concept of "sampling distribution." The first sampling distribution discussed by most texts is the sampling distribution of the mean. The problem with this approach is that the sampling distribution of the mean cannot be generated from simple probability considerations, which makes it hard for students to understand. This problem is compounded by the fact that most texts do not attempt to generate the sampling distribution of the mean in a concrete way. Rather, they define it theoretically, as a probability distribution that would result if an infinite number of random samples of size N were taken from the population and the mean of each sample were calculated. This definition is far too abstract for students, especially when this is their initial contact the *idea* of sampling distributions. *When students fail to grasp the concept of sampling distributions, they fail to grasp the rest of inferential statistics.* What appears to happen is that since students do not understand the material conceptually, they are forced to memorize the equations and to solve problems rotely. Thus, students are often able to solve the problems without genuinely understanding what they are doing, all because they fail to comprehend the essence of sampling distributions.

To impart a basic understanding of sampling distributions, I believe it is far better to begin with the sign test (Chapter 10), a simple inference test for which the binomial distribution is the appropriate sampling distribution. The binomial distribution is very easy to understand, and it can be derived from the basic probability rules developed in an earlier chapter (Chapter 8, "Random Sampling and Probability"). It is entirely dependent on simple, logical considerations. Hence, students can easily follow its generation. Moreover, it can also be generated by the same empirical process that is used later in the text for generating the sampling distribution of the mean. It therefore serves as an important bridge to understanding all the sampling distributions discussed later in the textbook. Introducing hypothesis testing with the sign test has other advantages. All of the important concepts involving hypothesis testing can be illustrated (e.g., null hypothesis, alternative hypothesis, alpha level, Type I and Type II errors, and power). The sign test also provides an illustration of the before-after (repeated measures) design, which is a superior way to begin, as most students are familiar with this type of experiment, and the logic of the design is quite easy to follow.

Chapter 11 discusses power. Many texts do not discuss power at all, or else leave it until near the end of the book. Power is a complicated topic. Using the sign test as the vehicle for a power analysis simplifies matters. Understanding power is necessary if one is to grasp the methodology of scientific investigation itself. When students gain insight into power, they can see why we bother discussing Type II errors. Further, they see for the first time why we conclude by "retaining H_0" as a reasonable explanation of the data rather than by "accepting H_0 as true" (a most important distinction). In this same vein, students also appreciate the error involved when one concludes that two conditions are equal from data that are not statistically significant. Thus, power is a topic that brings the whole hypothesis testing methodology into sharp focus.

At this state of the exposition, a diligent student can grasp the idea that data analysis basically involves two steps: (1) calculating the appropriate statistic and (2) evaluating the statistic based on its sampling distribution. The time is ripe for a formal discussion of sampling distributions and how they can be generated (Chapter 12). After this, the sampling distribution of the mean is introduced. Rather than depending on an abstract theoretical definition of the sampling distribution of the mean, the text discusses how this sampling distribution can be generated empirically. This gives a much more concrete understanding of the sampling distribution of the mean.

Due to previous experience with one easily understood sampling distribution, the binomial distribution, and using the empirical approach for the sampling distribution of the mean, most conscientious students have a good grasp of what sampling distributions are and why they are essential for inferential statistics. Since the sampling distributions underlying Student's *t* test and the analysis of variance are also explained in terms of their empirical generation, students can understand the use of these tests rather than just rotely solving problems. With this background, students can comprehend that all of the concepts of hypothesis testing are the same as we go from statistic to statistic. What varies from experiment to experiment is the statistic used and its accompanying sampling distribution. The stage is set for moving through the remaining inference tests.

Chapters 12, 13, 14, and 18 discuss, in a fairly conventional way, the *z* test and *t* test for single samples, the *t* test for correlated and independent groups, and nonparametric statistics. However, these chapters differ from those in other textbooks in the clarity of presentation, the number and interest value of fully solved problems, and the implementing the new teaching method, we would want to know how much better the new teaching method is, that is, how large is the effect. Most probably, we would be very hesitant to make the investment if the size of the effect was quite small, say, only a few percentage points in end-of-course performance. On the other hand, if the effect were a large one, assuming other factors were favorable, it could make sense to bite the bullet and incorporate the new teaching method into the curriculum.

Because of the importance of this topic, we have decided to include it in the sixth edition. "Size of Effect" is discussed generally in conjunction with power in Chapter 11 and specifically in conjunction with the *t* test for independent groups in Chapter 14 and the analysis of variance in Chapter 15.

- Including the Topic, "Effect of Extreme Score" in Chapter 6, "Correlation." This section alerts the student to the rather large effect that an extreme score can have on the value of the correlation coefficient, particularly when *N* is small. Accordingly, the student is cautioned to check the scatter plot for extreme scores when computing correlation coefficients.

- Two New "What Is The Truth?" Sections. A new "What Is The Truth?" section has been added at the end of Chapter 8, entitled, "A Sample of a Sample." This section discusses how representative samples for polls are formed, using the New York Times/CBS News Poll as an example. Another new "What Is The Truth?" section has been added at the end of Chapter 10, entitled "Anecdotal Reports Versus Systematic Research." This section queries the students about an article that appeared in a recent issue of the *New York Times on the Web*. The article presents an important and fairly common occurrence in real life, namely, a situation where testimony from individuals about the effectiveness of a product is in conflict with systematic research concerning the product.

- New or Revised End-of-Chapter Questions and Problems. More than 30 new or revised end-of-chapter questions and problems have been added to update and extend this material.

- New Web-Based End-of-Chapter Section, "WEB CONNECTION." In the sixth edition, there is a new section at the end of each chapter that alerts students that the following new Web-based material for that chapter is available for their use:

  1. An on-line quiz to test their knowledge before moving on. These quizzes exist for each chapter and are located at http:\\psychology.wadsworth.com\courses\statistics.

  2. Additional on-line, fully solved practice problems for the chapter. If they desire, students can get more practice in solving problems appropriate for the chapter material by doing these practice problems. There are additional, fully solved Practice Problems for each chapter; they are located at http:\\psychology.wadsworth.com\courses\statistics.

- Adding Chapter Outlines. Chapter outlines have been added at the beginning of each chapter to help the student preview the forthcoming material.

- Wording and Formatting Changes. Minor wording and formatting changes have been made throughout the textbook to improve clarity and interest.

Ancillary Package The supplements consist of:

- A **student's study guide** that is intended for review and consolidation of the material contained in each chapter of the textbook. Each chapter of the study guide has a chapter outline, a programmed learning concept review, exercises and answers to exercises, true-false questions and answers, and an end-of-chapter self-quiz with answers. Many students have commented on the helpfulness of this study guide.
- This **instructor's manual,** which contains short answer, multiple choice, and true-false questions for each chapter. The answers to the multiple choice and true-false questions are given in bold type to the left of the question. This manual also contains answers to selected end-of-chapter problems contained in the textbook. Because of requests from instructors, I have not included answers to *all* the computational end-of-chapter problems found in the text; instead, I have omitted answers from at least one problem in each chapter. These answers are found at the end of the instructor's manual. This manual also contains end-of-chapter problems suitable for computer use (see below).
- **Software:** The **MINITAB Manual** that accompanied the fifth edition has been discontinued because of low demand. The end-of-chapter computer problems contained in the MINITAB manual have been placed in the instructor's manual for instructors to use as desired. For instructors who desire to use SPSS in conjunction with their statistics course, I recommend L. A. Kirkpatrick and B. C. Feeney, *A Simple Guide to SPSS for Windows for Versions 8.0 & 9.0, Revised Edition,* Wadsworth/Thomson Learning, Belmont, CA, 2000.
- **ExamView,** a computerized testing package for Windows or Macintosh computers that allows instructors to create, edit, store, and print exams.

The material covered in this textbook, study guide, and instructor's manual is appropriate for undergraduate students with a major in psychology or related behavioral science discipline. I believe the approach I have followed helps considerably to impart this subject matter with understanding. I am grateful to receive any feedback that will improve the quality of these materials. Please send your comments to the web master at http://psychology.wadsworth.com/.

Fort Collins, Colorado
October, 2000

Robert R. Pagano

CHAPTER 1

STATISTICS AND SCIENTIFIC METHOD

Multiple Choice Questions

Refer to the following information in answering questions 1 - 8.

Let's assume you are conducting an experiment to determine the effect of a new drug on the incidence of epileptic seizures. You select 20 epileptics from the 150 epileptics being treated at a nearby hospital and administer the drug to them. You record the number of seizures in each of the 20 subjects for one month.

d 1. The new drug is an example of a(n) _________.

a. dependent variable
b. constant
c. statistic
d. independent variable

a 2. The number of seizures for each subject is an example of a(n) _________.

a. dependent variable
b. constant
c. statistic
d. independent variable

b 3. The 20 subjects constitute a _________.

a. population
b. sample
c. parameter
d. cannot answer without more information

a 4. The 150 epileptics constitute a ___________.

a. population
b. sample
c. parameter
d. need more information

d 5. The number of seizures for each of the 20 subjects are called _________.

a. constants
b. statistics
c. parameters
d. data

d 6. The number of seizures for each of the 150 epileptics are called _________.

a. constants
b. statistics
c. parameters
d. data

b 7. The average (mean) number of seizures for the 20 subjects is called a _________.

a. constant
b. statistic
c. parameter
d. sample

c 8. The average (mean) number of seizures for the 150 epileptics would be called a _________.

a. constant
b. statistic
c. parameter
d. sample

For questions 9 - 14, refer to the following information.

In order to estimate the average (mean) weight of all professional football players, an investigator determines the weight of the "Dallas Cowboy" players.

d 9. Weight is an example of a(n) _________.

a. independent variable
b. constant
c. statistic
d. dependent variable

b 10. The weight of each Dallas Cowboy is called ___________.

a. constants
b. data
c. parameters
d. statistics

c 11. The Dallas Cowboys are a _________.

a. population
b. parameter
c. sample
d. statistic

a 12. All professional football players constitute a _________.

a. population
b. parameter
c. sample
d. statistic

d 13. The average (mean) weight of the Dallas Cowboys is called a _________.

a. population
b. parameter
c. sample
d. statistic

b 14. The average (mean) weight of all professional football players is called a _________.

a. population
b. parameter
c. sample
d. statistic

a 15. In order to estimate the amount of TV watched by New York City adults, a sociologist surveys a random sample of adults from this city. The obtained raw scores are called _________.

a. data
b. constants
c. statistics
d. populations

c 16. In question 15, the average (mean) of the raw scores is a _________.

a. population
b. sample
c. statistic
d. parameter

a 17. In question 15, all New York City adults constitute a _________.

a. population
b. sample
c. statistic
d. parameter

b 18. Let's assume you have measured the height of all psychology majors at your university. The resulting raw scores are called _________.

a. constants
b. data
c. coefficients
d. statistics

c 19. In question 18, height is an example of a(n) _________.

a. independent variable
b. constant
c. dependent variable
d. statistic

a 20. In question 18, the height scores constitute a _________ with regard to psychology majors at your university.

a. population
b. sample
c. parameter
d. statistic

b 21. In question 18, the height scores constitute a _________ with regard to psychology majors in universities throughout the world.

a. population
b. sample
c. parameter
d. statistic

c 22. In question 18, the average (mean) value of the height scores constitutes a _________ with regard to psychology majors at your university.

a. population
b. sample
c. parameter
d. statistic

d 23. In question 18, the average (mean) value of the height scores constitutes a _________ with regard to psychology majors at universities throughout the world.

a. population
b. sample
c. parameter
d. statistic

c 24. In order to estimate the attention level of college undergraduates in the United States, a psychologist measures the attention span of the undergraduates at a local university. The mean of these scores is a _________.

a. parameter
b. population
c. statistic
d. sample

c 25. In question 24, the undergraduates at the local university are a _________.

a. parameter
b. population
c. sample
d. statistic

d 26. In order to estimate the ratio of white to black student in his college, a professor determines the proportion of whites and blacks in his class. The resulting proportion is called a _________.

a. population
b. sample
c. parameter
d. statistic

a 27. In problem 26, the students in the professor's class are called a _________.

a. sample
b. population
c. statistic
d. parameter

b 28. In problem 26, the students of the entire college are called a _________.

a. sample
b. population
c. statistic
d. parameter

e 29. Inferential statistics _________.

a. is the same as descriptive statistics
b. also uses methods of descriptive statistics
c. allows one to make inferences about a sample based on population data
d. allows one to make inferences about a population based on sample data
e. b and d

e 30. Descriptive statistics are used to _________.

a. calculate the mean and standard deviation of a sample
b. calculate the mean and standard deviation of a population
c. graph a distribution of raw scores
d. b and c
e. a, b and c

e 31. In the equation $Y = bX + a$, b is a(n) _________.

a. independent variable
b. dependent variable
c. constant
d. coefficient
e. c and d

Short Answer Questions

1. A developmental psychologist conducts an experiment to determine if exposure to an enriched environment shortly after birth will cause increased brain development. Twenty, two month old rats are randomly selected from a pool of one thousand, two-month-old, rat pups. Ten of the twenty pups are exposed to an enriched environment for three weeks and the other ten to the usual environment for the same period of time. At a suitable time after the exposure, the psychologist measures the number of neurons per cm^3 in the brain of each rat. A comparison is then made of the mean number of neurons per cm^3 for each group. Identify the following:

a. The population
b. The sample
c. The independent variable
d. The dependent variable
e. Any statistics

2. Compare the method of authority with scientific method.

3. What is the major difference between descriptive and inferential statistics? Illustrate, using an example.

True-False Questions

T 1. A sample is a subset of a population.

F 2. The dependent variable is the variable that is systematically manipulated.

F 3. The independent variable is the variable that is measured to determine the effect of the independent variable.

T 4. A statistic is to a sample as a parameter is to a population.

T 5. Descriptive statistics involves characterizing the obtained data.

T 6. Inferential statistics uses the sample data to generalize to populations.

F 7. Observational studies involve the manipulation of variables by the investigator.

T 8. True experiments involve the manipulation of variables by the investigator.

F 9. Observational studies involve the use of independent variables

CHAPTER 2

BASIC MATHEMATICAL AND MEASUREMENT CONCEPTS

Multiple Choice Questions

b 1. Given the following subjects and scores, which symbol would be used to represent the score of 3?

Subject	1	2	3	4	5
Score	12	21	8	3	30

a. X_8
b. X_4
c. X_3
d. X_2

d 2. We have collected the following data:

$$X_1 = 6, X_2 = 2, X_3 = 4, X_4 = 1, X_5 = 3$$

For these data, $\sum_{i=1}^{N-1} X_i$ is equal to ________.

a. 16
b. 10
c. 7
d. 13

a 3. Reaction time in seconds is an example of a(n) ________ scale.

a. ratio
b. ordinal
c. interval
d. nominal

b 4. After performing several clever calculations on your calculator, the display shows the answer 53.655001. What is the appropriate value rounded to two decimal places?

a. 53.65
b. 53.66
c. 53.64
d. 53.60

d 5. Consider the following points on a scale:

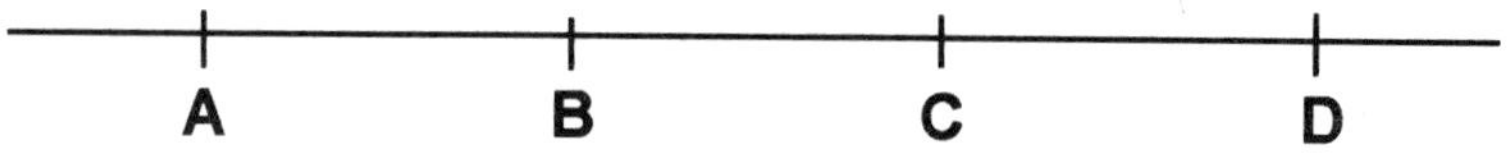

If the scale upon which *A*, *B*, *C*, and *D* are arranged is a nominal scale, we can say __________.

a. $B = 2A$
b. $B - A = D - C$
c. both a and b
d. neither a nor b

c 6. When rounded to two decimal places, the number 3.175000 becomes __________.

a. 3.17
b. 3.20
c. 3.18
d. 3.10

d 7. Given the data $X_1 = 1$, $X_2 = 4$, $X_3 = 5$, $X_4 = 8$, $X_5 = 10$, evaluate ΣX.

a. 1
b. 18
c. 27
d. 28

c 8. Given the above data of question 7, evaluate ΣX^2.

a. 56
b. 784
c. 206
d. 28

b 9. Given the data of question 7, evaluate $(\Sigma X)^2$.

a. 56
b. 784
c. 206
d. 28

a 10. Given the data of question 7, evaluate $\sum_{i=2}^{4} X_i$.

a. 17
b. 27
c. 28
d. 23

d 11. Given the data of question 7, evaluate $\sum_{i=2}^{N} X_i + 5$.

a. 53
b. 47
c. 48
d. 32

a 12. Given the data of question 7, evaluate $\sum_{i=2}^{N} (X_i + 5)$.

a. 47
b. 53
c. 48
d. 32

b 13. A discrete scale of measurement _________.

a. is the same as a continuous scale
b. provides exact measurements
c. necessarily uses whole numbers
d. b and c

b 14. Consider the following points on a scale:

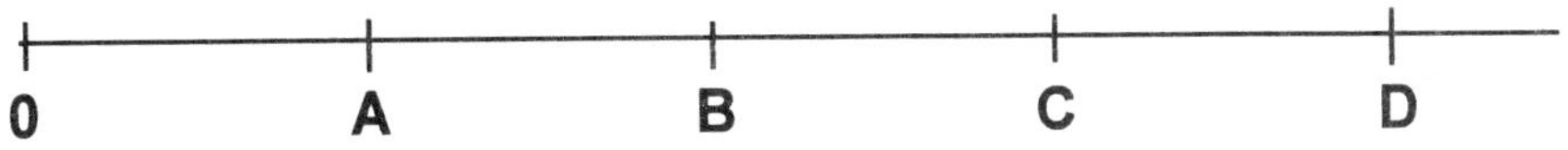

If the scale upon which *A*, *B*, *C*, and *D* are arranged is an interval scale, we can say _________.

a. $B = 2A$
b. $B - A = D - C$
c. both a and b
d. neither a nor b

c 15. The number 83.476499 rounded to three decimal places is _________.

a. 83.477
b. 83.480
c. 83.476
d. 83.470

a 16. The number 9.44650 rounded to two decimal places is _________.

a. 99.45
b. 99.46
c. 99.44
d. 99.40

a 17. "Brand of soft drink" is measured on a(n) _________.

a. nominal scale
b. ordinal scale
c. interval scale
d. ratio scale

b 18. At the annual sailing regatta, prizes are awarded for 1st, 2nd, 3rd, 4th, and 5th place. These "places" comprise a(n) _________.

a. nominal scale
b. ordinal scale
c. interval scale
d. ratio scale

c 19. Which of the following numbers is rounded incorrectly to two decimal places?

a. 10.47634 → 10.48
b. 15.36485 → 15.36
c. 21.47500 → 21.47
d. 8.24501 → 8.25
e. 6.66500 → 6.66

d 20. Consider the following points on a scale:

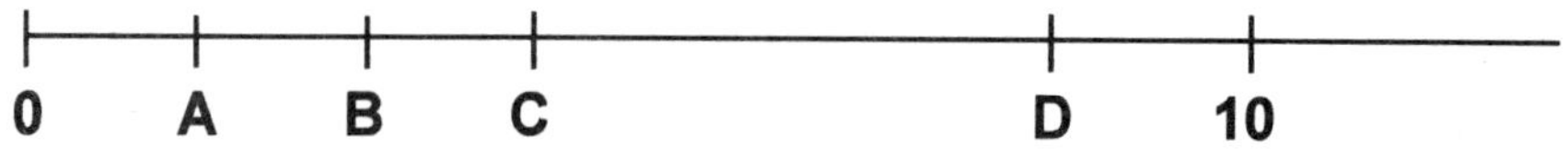

If the scale upon which points *A*, *B*, *C*, and *D* are shown is an ordinal scale, we can meaningfully say _________.

a. $B - A < D - C$
b. $B < C/2$
c. $B = 2A$
d. $C > B$

e 21. A continuous scale of measurement is different than a discrete scale in that a continuous scale _________.

a. is an interval scale, not a ratio scale
b. never provides exact measurements
c. can take an infinite number of intermediate possible values
d. never uses decimal numbers
e. b and c

b 22. Sex of children is an example of a(n) _________ scale.

a. ratio
b. nominal
c. ordinal
d. interval

d 23. Which of the following variables has been labeled with an incorrect measuring scale?

a. the <u>number of students</u> in a psychology class - ratio
b. <u>ranking</u> in a beauty contest - ordinal
c. <u>finishing order</u> in a poetry contest - ordinal
d. <u>self-rating of anxiety level</u> by students in a statistics class - ratio

c 24. A nutritionist uses a scale that measures weight to the nearest 0.01 grams. A slice of cheese weighs 0.35 grams on the scale. The variable being measured is a _________.

a. discrete variable
b. constant
c. continuous variable
d. random variable

b 25. In question 24, the true weight of the cheese _________.

a. is 0.35 grams
b. may be anywhere in the range 0.345-0.355 grams
c. may be anywhere in the range 0.34-0.35 grams
d. may be anywhere in the range 0.34-0.36 grams

a 26. In a 10-mile cross-country race, all runners are randomly assigned an identification number. These numbers represent a(n) _________.

a. nominal scale
b. ratio scale
c. interval scale
d. ordinal scale

b 27. In the race mentioned in question 26, a comparison of each runner's finishing time would represent a(n) _________.

a. nominal scale
b. ratio scale
c. interval scale
d. ordinal scale

b 28. The sum of a distribution of 40 scores is 150. If we add a constant of 5 to each score, the resulting sum will be _________.

a. 158
b. 350
c. 150
d. 195

Short Answer Questions

1. How does an interval scale differ from an ordinal scale?

2. Give two differences between continuous and discrete scales.

3. What are the four types of scales and what mathematical operations can be done with each?

4. Prove algebraically that $\sum_{i=1}^{N}(X_i + a) = \sum_{i=1}^{N} X_i + Na$.

True-False Questions

T 1. When doing summation, the number above the summation sign indicates the term ending the summation and the number below indicates the beginning term.

F 2. ΣX^2 and $(\Sigma X)^2$ generally yield the same answer.

F 3. With nominal scales there is a numerical relationship between the units of the scale.

T 4. If IQ was measured on a ratio scale, and John had an IQ of 40 and Fred an IQ of 80, it would be correct to say that Fred was twice as intelligent as John.

F 5. An ordinal scale possesses the attributes of magnitude and equal interval.

F 6. Most scales used for measuring psychological variables are either ratio or interval.

T 7. Measurement is always approximate with a continuous variable.

F 8. It is standard practice to carry all intermediate calculations to four more decimal places than will be reported in the final answer.

T 9. In rounding, if the remainder beyond the last digit is greater than 1/2, add one to the last digit. If the remainder is less than 1/2, leave the last digit as it is.

CHAPTER 3

FREQUENCY DISTRIBUTIONS

Multiple Choice Questions

For questions 1 - 6, refer to the following information.

A psychologist is interested in the social interactions of preschool children. She measures the number of verbal interactions that each child at a preschool engages in during a day. Here is the frequency distribution of the data.

Class interval	Frequency
96-105	5
86-95	4
76-85	6
66-75	7
56-65	10
46-55	4
36-45	3
26-35	3
16-25	2
6-15	1

b 1. The real limits of the interval 56-65 are _________.

a. 56.5-65.5
b. 55.5-65.5
c. 55-67
d. 56-65

a 2. The relative frequency for the interval 76-85 is _________.

a. 0.13
b. 0.09
c. 0.16
d. 0.11

d 3. The cumulative frequency for the interval 46-55 is _________.

a. 4
b. 9
c. 0.29
d. 13

d 4. The cumulative % for the interval 46-55 is _________.

a. 8.89%
b. 20.00%
c. 0.64%
d. 28.89%

a 5. The percentile rank of a score of 40 is _________.

a. 16.33%
b. 16.00%
c. 9.67%
d. 16.67%

c 6. The 50th percentile point is _________.

a. 65.50
b. 62.15
c. 65.00
d. 74.00

For questions 7 - 12, refer to the following information.

A researcher has collected some data on the amount of time in seconds (to the nearest 0.1 second) that it took trained rats to run through a maze. The data is shown below arranged in a frequency distribution of grouped scores.

Class interval	Frequency
7.6-7.9	3
7.2-7.5	1
6.8-7.1	6
6.4-6.7	6
6.0-6.3	3
5.6-5.9	4
5.2-5.5	5
4.8-5.1	4
4.4-4.7	1
4.0-4.3	3

c 7. The real limits of the interval 6.4-6.7 are _________.

a. 6.3-6.8
b. 6.4-6.7
c. 6.35-6.75
d. 6.45-6.75

b 8. The relative frequency for the interval 5.2-5.5 is _________.

a. 0.03
b. 0.14
c. 0.11
d. 13

a 9. The cumulative frequency for the interval 6.0-6.3 is _________.

a. 20
b. 0.57
c. 17
d. 57

d 10. The cumulative percentage for the interval 5.2-5.5 is _________.

a. 13.89%
b. 47.22%
c. 22.22%
d. 36.11%

a 11. The percentile rank of a score of 6.5 is _________.

a. 61.81%
b. 59.72%
c. 9.37%
d. 9.03%

c 12. The 75th percentile point is _________.

a. 6.42
b. 6.87
c. 6.82
d. 6.47

For questions 13 - 16, refer to the following information.

Group the raw scores given below into a frequency distribution of approximately 12 intervals of equal width.

58	70	68	59	62
47	90	57	45	68
93	83	45	48	55
32	58	36	63	71
60	41	65	84	42
40	87	75	81	80
61	72	76	73	52
80	61	80	70	51
63	71	94	66	68
69	60	61		

d 13. The value of *i* is _________.

a. 5.5
b. 4
c. 6
d. 5

d 14. The lowest class interval is _________.

a. 30-35
b. 32-36
c. 32-37
d. 30-34

b 15. The highest frequency for any interval is _________.

a. 6
b. 8
c. 10
d. 7

a 16. The interval containing the most scores is _________.

a. 60-64
b. 62-66
c. 62-67
d. 60-65

b 17. The distribution of scores of high school seniors on a sixth grade math test would probably be _________.

a. positively skewed
b. negatively skewed
c. normal
d. symmetrical but not normal

a 18. If a large psychology class took a test on theoretical biophysics, the distribution of scores would probably be _________.

a. positively skewed
b. symmetrical
c. negatively skewed
d. ogival

c 19. An accountant is preparing a graph showing the number of sports cars of various makers purchased this year. The number will be plotted on the ordinate and the various manufacturers on the abscissa. The proper type of graph for this data is a(n) _________.

a. frequency polygon
b. histogram
c. bar graph
d. ogive

c 20. If a curve is symmetrical, _________.

a. most of the scores fall at the lower values of the *X* axis
b. most of the scores fall at the higher values of the *X* axis
c. if folded in half, the two sides of the curve coincide
d. most of the scores fall at the higher values of the *Y* axis

d 21. Interval or ratio data may be plotted as a _________.

a. bar graph
b. histogram
c. frequency polygon
d. b and c

d 22. Your new Mercedes weighs 1850 kilograms when measured to the nearest kilogram. The real limits of its weight are _________.

a. 1800-1900
b. 1840-1860
c. 1849-1851
d. 1849.5-1850.5

Short Answer Questions

1. Compare and contrast a histogram and a bar graph.

2. Give an example of a histogram. Be sure to label the axes and the variable plotted.

3. Construct a stem and leaf diagram of the distribution of raw scores given on page 20.

True-False Questions

T 1. In grouping scores, the wider the intervals, the more information that is lost.

T 2. In constructing a frequency distribution of grouped scores, the intervals must be continuous and mutually exclusive.

F 3. Any percentile point for a distribution of scores must have a value equal to one of the scores.

F 4. A histogram is like a bar graph except with a histogram the bars don't touch each other.

T 5. A frequency polygon results in a curve that looks as though the scores were continuously distributed.

T 6. If a curve is negatively skewed, most of the scores occur at the higher values and the curve tails off toward the lower end of the horizontal axis.

F 7. A bell shaped curve is an example of a skewed distribution.

F 8. In constructing a frequency distribution of grouped scores, *i* should be rounded to one more decimal place than in the raw scores.

F 9. All frequency distributions are of grouped scores.

T 10. The percentile rank of a score is equal to the percentage of scores in the distribution that fall below the score in question.

CHAPTER 4

MEASURES OF CENTRAL TENDENCY AND VARIABILITY

Multiple Choice Questions

For questions 1 - 6, refer to the following information.

An industrial psychologist observed 8 drill-press operators for one working day. She recorded the number of times each operator pressed the "faster" button instead of the "stop" button to determine whether the design of the control panel was contributing to the high rate of accidents in the plant. The resulting scores were as follows:

5, 2, 8, 2, 3, 2, 4, 12

a 1. The mode for this distribution is _________.

a. 2
b. 3
c. 8
d. there is no mode

b 2. The median is _________.

a. 2.00
b. 3.50
c. 3.00
d. 3.25

c 3. The mean is _________.

a. 3.52
b. 5.43
c. 4.75
d. 4.15

b 4. The range is _________.

a. 9
b. 10
c. 12
d. 2

d 5. The standard deviation is _________. Assume sample data.

a. 3.34
b. 5.81
c. 2.28
d. 3.58

c 6. The variance is _________. Assume sample data.

a. 33.75
b. 11.19
c. 12.79
d. 15.75

For questions 7 - 12, refer to the following information.

A history professor gives a quiz to his class and records the following scores:

13, 11, 11, 9, 12, 13, 16, 14, 11, 10, 8, 13, 20.

c 7. The mode(s) for this distribution is(are) _________.

a. 11
b. 13
c. 11 and 13
d. there is no mode

a 8. The median is _________.

a. 12
b. 11
c. 13
d. 16

a 9. The mean is _________.

a. 12.38
b. 13.42
c. 18.05
d. 11.50

b 10. The range is _________.

a. 13
b. 12
c. 8
d. 20

a 11. The standard deviation is _________. Assume sample scores.

a. 3.12
b. 3.00
c. 13.26
d. 12.74

c 12. The variance is _________. Assume sample scores.

a. 162.38
b. 9.01
c. 9.76
d. 9.60

d 13. Consider the following scores: 21, 22, 22, 0.1, 20, 25, 28, 26, 23, 19, 0.5. Which of the measures listed below would give the best description of the central tendency of these scores?

a. mean
b. variance
c. range
d. median

c 14. The mean weight for team *A* with 15 members is 140 lbs., the mean weight for team *B* with 7 members is 135 lbs., and the mean weight for team *C* with 20 members is 160 lbs. The overall mean weight for all three teams is _________.

a. 145.00
b. 138.78
c. 148.69
d. 178.43

c 15. Let's assume that we have determined the salary of all the professors at your school. In plotting the distribution of salaries we notice that it is positively skewed. For this distribution _________.

a. mean = median
b. mean < median
c. mean > median
d. can't tell from the information given

a 16. For any distribution of scores $\Sigma(X-\mu)$ = _________.

a. 0
b. ΣX
c. 1
d. $\overline{X}$

b 17. A distribution has a mean of 78 and a median of 92. This distribution is _________.

a. symmetrical
b. negatively skewed
c. positively skewed
d. not enough information given

b 18. In a certain statistics course, four exams were given. Each student's grade was based on a weighted average of his exam scores. The first two tests had weights of 1, the third test had a weight of 2, and the final test had a weight of 3. The exam scores for one student are listed below.

Exam	Grade
1	75.2
2	78.4
3	85.8
4	93.3

The student's overall average was _________.

a. 151.28
b. 86.44
c. 83.18
d. 47.52

c 19. On a physics exam, the instructor gives a bonus question worth 10 points. The class average (mean) without counting the bonus question is 83. If everyone gets the bonus question correct, the class mean would _________.

a. remain the same
b. equal 83 + 10/*N*
c. equal 93
d. exceed the median

a 20. The most commonly encountered measure of central tendency is the _________.

a. mean
b. median
c. mode
d. standard deviation

d 21. Which of the following is not a property of the mean?

a. The mean is sensitive to the exact value of all the scores.
b. The sum of the deviations about the mean equals zero.
c. The sum of the squared deviations about the mean is a minimum.
d. The mean is most subject to sampling variation.
e. The mean is most affected by extreme scores.

c 22. If the distribution is symmetrical, which is the best measure of central tendency?

a. mode
b. median
c. mean
d. variance

a 23. In a bell-shaped distribution, _________.

a. median = mean
b. median > mean
c. median < mean
d. standard deviation equals variance

c 24. If a constant of 5 is subtracted from all of the scores, the standard deviation _________.

a. decreases by 5
b. decreases by $\sqrt{5/N}$
c. remains the same
d. decreases by 5/*N*

e 25. Which of the following is not a measure of variability?

a. standard deviation
b. range
c. sum of squares
d. variance
e. all of the above are measures of variability

d 26. Which of the following do (does) not measure <u>average</u> dispersion?

a. standard deviation
b. range
c. sum of squares
d. b and c

b 27. In calculating the standard deviation of a sample, we use _________ in the denominator.

a. *N*
b *N* – 1
c. The sum of the weights
d *X*

b 28. The most commonly encountered measure of variability is _________.

a. range
b. standard deviation
c. mean
d. mode

f 29. Which of the following is (are) not true?

a. μ stands for the mean of a population
b. σ stands for the standard deviation of a population
c. *s* stands for the standard deviation of a sample
d. $\overline{X}$ stands for the mean of a sample
e. σ^2 stands for the variance of a population
f. all of the above

c 30. If 10 points were added to each score in a distribution, which of the following will happen?

a. the mean will remain unchanged
b. the mode will remain unchanged
c. the standard deviation will be unchanged
d. the mean, median, and mode will remain unchanged
e. c and d are both correct

Short Answer Questions

1. Compare and contrast the mean, median, and mode with respect to a) their sensitivity to extreme scores and b) their subjectivity to sampling variation.
2. Why do we divide by $N - 1$ in computing the standard deviation of a sample?
3. Which is a better measure of variability, the variance or the standard deviation? Explain.
4. Is the overall mean a weighted mean? Explain.

True-False Questions

F 1. In general, $\Sigma X^2 = (\Sigma X)^2$

F 2. The overall mean does not take into account the different number of subjects in each group.

F 3. The mode is used extensively in the behavioral sciences.

T 4. It is possible to have a set of scores with three different values for central tendency.

T 5. The median and the 50th percentile rank score will always have the same value.

T 6. The overall mean is a weighted mean.

F 7. When calculating the population standard deviation, we use $N - 1$ in the denominator.

F 8. The median is most affected by unbalanced extreme scores.

T 9. The equation for the sum of squares of a sample is $SS = \Sigma X^2 - (\Sigma X)^2/N$

F 10. Central tendency and variability are synonymous.

T 11. Central tendency describes the central location of the set of scores.

F 12. A deviation score is the same thing as a raw score.

T 13. We use $N - 1$ in the denominator of the equation for calculating the sample standard deviation because it provides us with an accurate estimate of the population standard deviation.

T 14. The mean is the arithmetic average of the scores.

F 15. If the number of raw scores is odd, the median is always the score in the middle position.

F 16. The median is less subject to sampling variation than the mean.

F 17. The mean must have a value equal to one of the scores in the distribution.

T 18. In a bell-shaped distribution, the mean, median and mode will be equal.

T 19. Variability and dispersion mean the same thing.

T 20. The range is equal to the highest score minus the lowest score.

F 21. The equation for standard deviation is the same regardless of whether the scores are of a sample or a population.

F 22. The variance is the square root of the standard deviation.

T 23. The mean is more often used for inference than the median.

F 24. If the distribution contains unbalanced extreme scores, the mean is a better descriptor than the median.

T 25. With grouped scores, the mode is the mid-point of the interval with the highest frequency.

F 26. In a skewed distribution, the mean and median are equal.

F 27. For data that are not normally distributed, the standard deviation will sometimes be negative.

CHAPTER 5

THE NORMAL CURVE AND STANDARD SCORES

Multiple Choice Questions

For questions 1 - 5, refer to the following information.

A stockbroker has kept a daily record of the value of a particular stock over the years and finds that prices of the stock form a normal distribution with a mean of $8.52 with a standard deviation of $2.38.

c 1. The percentile rank of a price of $13.87 is _________.

a. 48.78%
b. 1.22%
c. 98.78%
d. 51.22%

b 2. What percentage of the distribution lies between $5 and $11?

a. 21.48%
b. 78.41%
c. 49.41%
d. 57.98%

b 3. What percentage of the distribution lies below $7.42.

a. 17.72%
b. 32.28%
c. 82.28%
d. 31.92%

d 4. The stock price beyond which 0.05 of the distribution falls is _________.

a. $ 4.60
b. $12.47
c. $ 4.57
d. $12.44

a 5. The percentage of scores that lie between $9.00 and $10.00 is _________.

a. 15.31%
b. 31.17%
c. 23.24%
d. 7.93%

Questions 6 - 10 pertain to the following data.

A testing bureau reports that the mean for the population of Graduate Record Exam (GRE) scores is 500 with a standard deviation of 90. The scores are normally distributed.

d 6. The percentile rank of a score of 667 is _________.

a. 3.14%
b. 96.78%
c. 3.22%
d. 96.86%

c 7. The proportion of scores that lie above 650 is _________.

a. 0.4535
b. 0.9535
c. 0.0475
d. 0.0485

b 8. The proportion of scores that lie between 460 and 600 is _________.

a. 0.4394
b. 0.5365
c. 0.4406
d. 0.4635

a 9. The raw score that lies at the 90th percentile is _________.

a. 615.20
b. 384.80
c. 616.10
d. 383.90

d 10. The proportion of scores between 300 and 400 is _________.

a. 0.3665
b. 0.4868
c. 0.8533
d. 0.1203

a 11. The standard deviation of the *z* distribution equals _________.

a. 1
b. 0
c. ΣX
d. *N*

b 12. The mean of the *z* distribution equals _________.

a. 1
b. 0
c. ΣX
d. *N*

b 13. The *z* score corresponding to the mean of a raw score distribution equals _________.

a. the mean of the raw scores
b. 0
c. 1
d. *N*

c 14. The normal curve is _________.

a. linear
b. rectangular
c. bell-shaped
d. skewed

a 15. In a normal curve, the inflection points occur at _________.

a. $\mu \pm 1\sigma$
b. $\pm 1\sigma$
c. $\mu \pm 2\sigma$
d. μ

d 16. The z score corresponding to a raw score of 120 is _________.

a. 1.2
b. 2.0
c. 1.0
d. impossible to compute from the information given

Questions 17 - 21 pertain to the following information.

An economics test was given and the following sample scores were recorded:

Individual	A	B	C	D	E	F	G	H	I	J
Score	12	12	7	10	9	12	13	8	9	8

b 17. The mean of the distribution is _________.

a. 12.00
b. 10.00
c. 9.00
d. 8.00

c 18. The standard deviation of the distribution is _________.

a. 10.20
b. 2.10
c. 2.11
d. 10.74

b 19. The *z* score for individual *D* is _________.

a. 1
b. 0
c. 10
d. $\overline{X}$

d 20. The *z* score for individual *E* is _________.

a. 0.47
b. 9.00
c. 4.27
d. –0.47

c 21. The z score for individual *G* is _________.

a. –1.42
b. 13.00
c. 1.42
d. 6.16

Questions 22 - 25 pertain to the following information.

A distribution has a mean of 60.0 and a standard deviation of 4.3.

d 22. The raw score corresponding to a z score of 0.00 is _________.

a. 64.3
b. 14.0
c. 4.3
d. 60.0

a 23. The raw score corresponding to a z score of −1.51 is _________.

a. 53.5
b. 66.5
c. 66.4
d. 53.6

b 24. The raw score corresponding to a *z* score of 2.02 is _________.

a. 51.3
b. 68.7
c. 51.4
d. 68.6

c 25. If a population of scores is normally distributed, has a mean of 45 and a standard deviation of 6, the most extreme 5% of the scores lie beyond the score(s) of _________.

a. 35.13
b. 45.99
c. 56.76 and 33.24
d. 45.99 and 35.13

Short Answer Questions

1. List three characteristics of a *z* distribution.
2. Is a *z* distribution always normally shaped? Explain.
3. Does the *z* transformation result in a score having the same units of measurement as the raw score? Explain. Why is this advantageous?

True-False Questions

F 1. A *z* distribution always is normally shaped.

T 2. All standard scores are *z* scores.

T 3. A *z* score is a transformed score.

T 4. A *z* score designates how many standard deviations the raw score is above or below the mean.

T 5. The *z* distribution takes on the same shape as the raw scores.

T 6. z scores allow comparison of variables that are measured on different scales.

T 7. In a normal curve, the area contained between the mean and a score that is 2.30 standard deviations above the mean is 0.4893 of the total area.

F 8. The normal curve reaches the horizontal axis in 4 standard deviations above and below the mean.

T 9. For any *z* distribution of normally distributed scores, P_{50} is always equal to zero.

CHAPTER 6

CORRELATION

Multiple Choice Questions

c 1. Correlation and regression differ in that _________.

a. correlation is primarily concerned with the size and direction of relationships
b. regression is primarily used for prediction
c. both a and b are true
d. neither a nor b are true

b 2. A scatter plot _________.

a. has to do with electron scatter
b. is a graph of paired *X* and *Y* values
c. must be linear
d. is a frequency graph of *X* values

a 3. If a relationship is linear, _________.

a. the relation can be most accurately represented by a straight line
b. all the points fall on a curved line
c. the relationship is best represented by a curved line
d. all the points must fall on a straight line

d 4. In the equation $Y = bX + a$, *X* and *Y* are _________.

a. constants
b. statistics
c. population parameters
d. variables

d 5. In question 4, *b* is _________.

a. a constant
b. the slope of the line
c. the *Y* axis intercept
d. a and b
e. a variable

a 6. In question 4, a is _________.

a. a constant giving the value of the *Y* axis intercept
b. a constant giving the value of the slope of the line
c. a variable relating *X* to *Y*
d. a variable relating *Y* to *X*

c 7. In a positive relationship, _________.

a. as *X* increases, *Y* increases
b. as *X* decreases, *Y* decreases
c. a and b
d. as *X* increases, *Y* decreases

d 8. In a negative relationship, _________.

a. as *X* increases, *Y* increases
b. as *X* decreases, *Y* decreases
c. a and b
d. as *X* increases, *Y* decreases

b 9. In a positive relationship, _________.

a. b is negative
b. b is positive
c. a must be positive
d. a must be negative

d 10. In a negative relationship, _________.

a. b is positive
b. b can be either positive or negative
c. a must be negative
d. b is negative

a 11. In a perfect relationship, _________.

a. all the points fall on the line
b. none of the points fall on the line
c. some of the points fall on the line
d. the points form an ellipse around the line

b 12. In an imperfect relationship, _________.

a. all the points fall on the line
b. a relationship exists, but all of the points do not fall on the line
c. no relationship exists
d. a relationship exists, but none of the points can fall on the line

d 13. A relationship can be _________.

a. perfect
b. imperfect
c. nonexistant
d. a, b and c

a 14. The closer the points on a scatter diagram fall to the regression line, the _________ between the scores.

a. higher the correlation
b. lower the correlation
c. correlation doesn't change
d. need more information

e 15. Which of the following is (are) correct interpretation(s) of correlation? Correlation _________.

a. indicates the degree of the relationship between two variables
b. indicates a causal relationship between two variables
c. is useful in deciding which variables to manipulate in an experimental study
d. a and b
e. a and c
f. a, b and c

d **16.** The lowest degree of correlation shown below is _________.

a. 0.75
b. –0.33
c. –0.25
d. 0.15

c **17.** The correlation coefficient between heights from the ground of two people on the opposite ends of a seesaw would be _________.

a. 1.0
b. 0
c. –1.0
d. cannot tell without further information

d **18.** If the correlation between variables *X* and *Y* is 0.95, which of the following is true?

a. X is a cause of Y
b. Y is a cause of X
c. low scores on X are accompanied by high scores on Y
d. high scores on X are accompanied by high scores on Y
e. a and d

d 19. Y can be most accurately predicted from X if the correlation between X and Y is ________.

a. 0.80
b. 0.00
c. 0.45
d. –0.98

a 20. Which Pearson correlation coefficient shows the strongest relationship between two variables?

a. –0.80
b. 0.00
c. 0.75
d. 0.20
e. 0.03

e 21. Knowing nothing more than that IQ and memory scores are correlated 0.84, you could validly conclude that ________.

a. good memory causes high IQ
b. high IQ causes good memory
c. neither good memory nor high IQ cause each other
d. a third variable causes both good memory and high IQ
e. none of the above

c 22. When deciding which measure of correlation to employ with a specific set of data, you should consider ________.

a. whether the relationship is linear or nonlinear
b. type of scale of measurement for each variable
c. a and b
d. none of the above

b 23. The proportion of variance accounted for by a correlation between two variables is determined by ________.

a. Y^2
b. r^2
c. r
d. b

b 24. Which of the following statements is true?

a. Correlation implies causation.
b. Causation implies correlation.
c. neither a nor b
d. both a and b

b 25. A correlation between college entrance exam grades and scholastic achievement was found to be –1.08. On the basis of this you would tell the university that _________.

a. the entrance exam is a good predictor of success
b. they should hire a new statistician
c. the exam is a poor predictor of success
d. students who do best on this exam will make the worst students
e. students are this school are underachieving

b 26. It is possible to compute a coefficient of correlation if one is given _________.

a. a single score
b. two sets of measurements on the same individuals
c. 50 scores of a clerical aptitude test
d. all of the above
e. none of the above

e 27. After several studies, Professor Smith concludes that there is a zero correlation between body weight and bad tempers. This means that _________.

a. heavy people tend to have bad tempers
b. skinny people tend to have bad tempers
c. no one has a bad temper
d. everyone has a bad temper
e. a person with a bad temper may be heavy or skinny

b 28. Which of the following statements concerning Pearson r is not true?

a. $r = 0.00$ represents the absence of a relationship.
b. The relationship between the two variables must be nonlinear.
c. $r = 0.76$ has the same predictive power as $r = -0.76$.
d. $r = 1.00$ represents a perfect relationship.
e. All of the above are true statements.

a 29. If the correlation between two variables is –1.00 and the score of a given individual is 2.20 standard deviations above the mean on one of the variables, we would predict a score on the second variable of _________.

a. 2.20 standard deviations below the mean
b. 2.20 standard deviations above the mean
c. more than 2.20 standard deviations above the mean
d. more than 2.20 standard deviations below the mean

e 30. Which of the following is (are) not correct interpretations of Pearson *r*?

a. ratio of the variability of *Y* to the variability of *X*
b. measure of extent to which paired scores occupy the same or opposite positions within their own distributions
c. difference between the variability of *Y* and the variability of *X*
d. square root of the proportion of the total variability of *Y* accounted for by *X*
e. a and c

e 31. Which of the following is (are) not correlation coefficients?

a. Pearson *r*
b. eta
c. rho
d. phi
e. they all are correlation coefficients

c 32. Rho is used ________.

a. when both variables are dichotomous
b. when both variables are of interval or ratio scaling
c. when one or both variables are only of ordinal scaling
d. when the data is nonlinear

b 33. When a correlation exists, lowering the range of either of the variables will ________.

a. raise the correlation
b. lower the correlation
c. not change the correlation
d. produce a causal relationship

b 34 A traffic safety officer conducted an experiment to determine whether there is a correlation between people's ages and driving speeds. Six individuals were randomly sampled and the following data were collected.

Age	20	25	45	46	60	65
Speed (mph)	60	47	55	38	45	35

The value of Pearson *r* equals ________.

a. –0.82
b. –0.70
c. –0.63
d. +0.70

a 35. In question 34, the proportion of variability of *Y* accounted for by *X* is _________.

a. 0.49
b. 0.67
c. 0.40
d. –0.49

b 36. A researcher wanted to know if the order in which runners finish a race is correlated with their weight. She conducts an experiment and the data are given below.

Finishing order	**1**	**2**	**3**	**4**	**5**	**6**
Weight (lbs)	**110**	**114**	**112**	**108**	**116**	**113**

What is the appropriate correlation coefficient for this data?

a. *r*
b. rho
c. phi
d. biserial

a 37. For the data in question 36, the correlation equals _________.

a. 0.31
b. 0.32
c. 0.41
d. 0.45

c. 38 If *N* is small, an extreme score _________.

a. won't affect r_{obt} unduly
b. should be thrown out
c. might have a large effect on r_{obt}
d. need more information

<u>Short Answer Questions</u>

1. Define the following: positive, negative, linear, curvilinear, perfect, and imperfect relationship.

2. Give two definitions of Pearson *r*.

3. Why is r^2 a useful statistic?

4. Why are *z* scores used, instead of raw scores, as the basis for determining Pearson *r*?

5. If the *N* is small, can an extreme score cause problems in interpreting the size of the relationship? Explain

True-False Questions

F 1. For a linear relationship to exist, all the points must fall on a straight line.

T 2. In a positive relationship as *X* increases, *Y* increases.

T 3. The slope of the line reveals whether the relationship is positive or negative.

T 4. The farther away the points on a scatter diagram fall from the regression line, the lower the correlation.

F 5. Correlation implies causation.

T 6. Causation implies correlation.

F 7. Given a –1.00 correlation coefficient, a raw score of 32 on one measure must be accompanied by a score of –32 on the corresponding second measure.

F 8. As the value of *r* increases, the proportion of variability of *Y* that is accounted for by *X* decreases.

T 9. r^2 is called the coefficient of determination.

T 10. Correlation deals with the relationship between two variables.

T 11. A correlation coefficient expresses quantitatively the degree of relationship between two variables.

T 12. In a perfect positive correlation, each individual obtains the same *z* score on each variable.

F 13. The range of a correlation coefficient is 0 to +1.

T 14. The use of *z* scores allows comparisons between variables measured on different scales and units.

T 15. Pearson r requires that the data be of interval or ratio scaling.

F 16. If the relationship is imperfect, the value of the correlation coefficient must be negative.

F 17. Rho is used where one or both variables are at least of interval scaling.

T 18. A scatter plot is used to help determine if the relationship is linear or curvilinear.

T 19. Spearman rho really derives from Pearson *r*.

F 20. In order to compute *r*, we must first convert each score to its *z* score and then do our calculations with the z scores.

F 21. Assuming a correlation exists, as the range of one of the variables decreases, *r* increases.

F 22. *r* decreases as *N* decreases.

CHAPTER 7

LINEAR REGRESSION

Multiple Choice Questions

a 1. The primary reason we use a scatter plot in linear regression is _________.

a. to determine if the relationship is linear or curvilinear
b. to determine the direction of the relationship
c. to compute the magnitude of the relationship
d. to determine the slope of the least squares regression line

d 2. When the relation between X and Y is imperfect, the prediction of Y given X is _________.

a. perfect
b. always equal to Y
c. impossible to determine
d. approximate

b 3. The regression equation most often used in psychology minimizes _________.

a. $\Sigma (Y - Y')$
b. $\Sigma (Y - Y')^2$
c. $\Sigma (Y - X)^2$
d. $\overline{D}$
e. none of the above

c 4. The regression of Y on X _________.

a. predicts X given Y
b. predicts X' given X
c. predicts Y given X
d. predicts Y given Y'

c 5. The regression of X on Y _________.

a. predicts Y given X
b. predicts Y given X
c. predicts X given Y
d. is generally the same as the regression of Y on X
e. c and d

b 6. If the correlation between two sets of scores is 0 and one had to predict the value of Y for any given value of X, the best prediction of Y would be ________.

a. b_Y
b. $\overline{Y}$
c. 0
d. $\overline{X}$

a 7. During the past 5 years there has been an inflationary trend. Listed below is the average cost of a gallon of milk for each year.

1981	1982	1983	1984	1985
$1.10	$1.23	$1.30	$1.50	$1.65

Assuming a linear relationship exists, and that the relationship continues unchanged through 1986, what would you predict for the average cost of a gallon of milk in 1986?

a. $1.77
b. $1.72
c. $1.70
d. $1.83

Questions 8 - 12 pertain to the following data

A researcher collects data on the relationship between the amount of daily exercise an individual gets and the percent body fat of the individual. The following scores are recorded.

Individual	1	2	3	4	5
Exercise (min)	10	18	26	33	44
% Fat	30	25	18	17	14

c 8. Assuming a linear relationship holds, the least squares regression line for predicting % fat from the amount of exercise an individual gets is ________.

a. $Y' = 0.476X + 33.272$
b. $Y' = 1.931X + 66.363$
c. $Y' = -0.476X + 33.272$
d. $Y' = -0.432X + 32.856$

d 9. If an individual exercises 20 minutes daily, his predicted % body fat would be _________.

a. 21.63
b. 27.74
c. 27.88
d. 23.75

a 10. The least squares regression line for predicting the amount of exercise from % fat is _________..

a. $X' = -1.931Y + 66.363$
b. $X' = -0.476Y + 33.272$
c. $X' = 1.931Y + 66.363$
d. $X' = -1.905Y + 62.325$

b 11. If an individual has 22% fat, his predicted amount of daily exercise is _________.

a. 22.80
b. 23.88
c. 24.76
d. 20.22

c 12. The value for the standard error of estimate in predicting % fat from daily exercise is _________.

a. 3.35
b. 4.32
c. 2.14
d. 1.66
e. none of above

c 13. The assumption of homoscedasticity is that _________.

a. the range of the *Y* scores is the same as the *X* scores
b. the *X* and *Y* distributions have the same mean values
c. the variability of *Y* doesn't change over the *X* scores
d. the variability of the *X* and *Y* distributions is the same

c 14. You go to a carnival and a sideshow performer wants to bet you $100 that he can guess your exact weight just from knowing your height. It turns out that there is the following relationship between height and weight.

Height (in)	**60.0**	**62.0**	**63.0**	**66.5**	**73.5**	**84.0**
Weight (lbs)	**99**	**107**	**111**	**125**	**153**	**195**

Should you accept the performers bet? Explain.

a. yes
b. need more information
c. no
d. yes, if he measures my height in centimeters

c 15. If $r = 0.4582$, $s_Y = 3.4383$, and $s_X = 5.2165$, the value of $b_Y =$ _________.

a. 0.695
b. 0.458
c. 0.302
d. 1 – 0.458
e. none of the above

b. 16. In multiple regression, if the second predictor variable correlates highly with the predicted variable, than it is quite likely that _________.

a. $R^2 = 1.00$
b. $R^2 > r^2$
c. $R^2 = r^2$
d. $R^2 < r^2$

Short Answer Questions

1. Why is it important to know the standard error of estimate for a set of paired scores?

2. Why does the least squares regression line minimize $\Sigma (Y - Y')^2$, rather than $\Sigma (Y - Y')$?

3. Is it true that, generally, the regression lines for predicting *Y* given *X* and *X* given *Y*, are not the same? Explain.

True-False Questions

F 1. The total error in prediction equals $\Sigma (Y - Y')$.

F 2. In general, the regression line for predicting *X* given *Y* is the same as the regression line for predicting *Y* given *X*.

F 3. An imperfect relationship generally yields exact prediction.

T 4. When the relationship is perfect, the regression of *Y* on *X* is the same as the regression of *X* on *Y*.

T 5. Properly speaking, we should limit our predictions to the range of the base data.

F 6. The least squares regression line insures the maximum number of direct hits.

T 7. To do linear regression, there must be paired scores on two variables.

T 8. If the standard deviations of the X and Y distributions are equal, then $r = b_Y$.

T 9. If $s_X = s_Y$ then $b_X = b_Y$.

F 10. The lower the r value, the lower the standard error of estimate.

T 11. Multiple regression uses more than one predictor variable.

CHAPTER 8

RANDOM SAMPLING AND PROBABILITY

Multiple Choice Questions

b 1. If events A and B are independent, then $p(A \text{ and } B)$ = _________.

a. $p(A) + p(B) - p(A \text{ and } B)$
b. $p(A)p(B)$
c. $p(A \text{ or } B)$
d. 0

b 2. If A and B are mutually exclusive and exhaustive, then $p(A \text{ and } B)$ = _________.

a. 1
b. 0
c. $p(A) + p(B)$
d. $p(A) + p(B) - p(A \text{ and } B)$

c 3. If the odds in favor of an event occurring are 9 to 1, the probability of the event occurring is _________.

a. 9
b. 1/9
c. 9/10
d. 8/9

d 4. Probabilities vary between _________.

a. 0 and 2
b. 0 and 100
c. –1 and 0
d. 0 and 1

a 5. The Addition Rule states _________.

a. $p(A \text{ or } B) = p(A) + p(B) - p(A \text{ and } B)$
b. $p(A \text{ and } B) = p(A)p(B|A)$
c. $P + Q = 1$
d. $p(A)p(B|A) = p(A)p(B)$

d 6. A sample is random if ________.

a. each possible sample of a given size has an equal chance of being selected
b. all members of the population have an equal chance of being selected into the sample
c. all members of the sample have an equal chance of being selected
d. a, or a and b
e. a and c

c 7. The Multiplication Rule states ________.

a. $p(A \text{ or } B) = p(A) + p(B) - p(A \text{ and } B)$
b. $p(A \text{ or } B) = p(A) + p(B)$
c. $p(A \text{ and } B) = p(A)p(B|A)$
d. $p(A \text{ and } B) = p(A) + p(B)$

a 8. *A priori* probability refers to ________.

a. a probability value deduced from reason alone
b. the highest priority probability
c. a probability value determined after collecting data
d. none of the above

c 9. *A posteriori* probability refers to ________.

a. a probability value deduced from reason alone
b. low priority probability
c. a probability value determined after collecting data
d. none of the above

b 10. Two events are mutually exclusive if ________.

a. they are independent
b. they both cannot occur together
c. the occurrence of one slightly alters the probability of occurrence of the other
d. the probability of their joint occurrence equals one

b 11. A set of events is exhaustive if ________.

a. the sum of their probabilities equals one
b. the set includes all of the possible events
c. they are mutually exclusive
d. they are independent

a 12. Two events are independent if _________.

a. the occurrence of one has no effect on the probability of occurrence of the other
b. the occurrence of one precludes the occurrence of the other
c. the occurrence of one substantially alters the probability of occurrence of the other
d. the sum of their probabilities equals one
e. a and d

b 13. Suppose you are going to randomly order individuals *A*, *B*, *C*, *D*, *E* and *F*. The probability the order will begin *A B* _ _ _ _ is _________.

a. 1.000
b. 0.033
c. 0.027
d. 0.000

d 14. A famous hypnotist performs in Meany Hall before a crowd of 350 students and 180 non-students. The hypnotist knows from previous experience that one-half of the students and two-thirds of the non-students are hypnotizable. What is the probability that a randomly chosen person from the audience will be hypnotizable or will be a non-student?

a. 0.330
b. 0.340
c. 0.869
d. 0.670

b 15. Captain Kirk and Mr. Spock are engaged in a 3-D backgammon playoff, a game employing 6 dice. Kirk asks Spock the probability of rolling the dice and observing 6 sixes. Assume the dice are not biased. Spock's correct *a priori* reply is _________.

a. "Insufficient data, Captain."
b. "One-sixth to the sixth power, Sir." Translation: $(1/6)^6$
c. "One-thirtysixth, Sir."
d. "One-thirtysix to the sixth power, Sir." $(1/36)^6$
e. "The probability is equal to (1/6)X(1/5)X(1/4)X(1/3)X (1/2)X(1/1), Sir." (1/720)

Questions 16 - 19 pertain to the following information.

A "hungry" undergraduate student was looking for a way of making some extra money. The student turned to a life of vice - gambling. To be a good gambler, he needed to know the probability of certain events. Help him out by answering the following questions.

a 16. The probability of drawing 3 aces in a row without replacement from a deck of 52 ordinary playing cards is _________.

a. 0.00018
b. 0.00046
c. 0.00017
d. 0.00045

b 17. The probability of drawing a face card (king, queen or jack) of any suit from a deck of 52 ordinary playing cards in one draw is _________.

a. 0.020
b. 0.231
c. 0.077
d. 0.019

c 18. The probability of drawing an ace, a king and a queen of any suit in that order is _________. Sampling is without replacement from a deck of 52 ordinary playing cards.

a. 0.00045
b. 0.00046
c. 0.00048
d. 0.00018

d 19. The probability of rolling "boxcars" (two sixes) with one roll of a pair of fair dice is _________.

a. 0.167
b. 0.333
c. 0.033
d. 0.028

b 20. A royal flush in poker is when you end up with the ace, king, queen, jack, and 10 of the same suit. It's the most rare event in poker. If you are playing with a well-shuffled, legitimate deck of 52 cards, what is the probability that if you are dealt 5 cards, you will have a royal flush? Assume randomness.

a. 0.0000000032
b. 0.000000013
c. 0.0000015
d. 0.0000004

Questions 21 - 24 pertain to the following information.

Let's assume you are having a party and have stocked your refrigerator with beverages. You have 12 bottles of Coors beer, 24 bottles of Rainier beer, 24 bottles of Schlitz light beer, 12 bottles of Hamms beer,

2 bottles of Heineken dark beer and 6 bottles of Pepsi soda. You go to the refrigerator to get beverages for your friends. In answering the following questions assume you are randomly sampling without replacement.

a 21. What is the probability the first beverage you get is a beer?

a. 0.9250
b. 0.9000
c. 0.9487
d. 0.7750

b 22. What is the probability the first bottle selected is a Coors beer?

a. 0.0750
b. 0.1500
c. 0.3000
d. 0.1622

b 23. What is the probability your first three bottles selected are Pepsi's?

a. 0.00044
b. 0.00024
c. 0.1875
d. 0.2250

a 24. What is the probability the first four bottles you select will be a Coors, a Schlitz, a Rainier, and a Coors in that order?

a. 0.0020
b. 0.0022
c. 0.8875
d. 0.0019

Questions 25 - 27 pertain to the following information.

Assume you are rolling two fair dice once.

c 25. The probability of obtaining a sum of 5 equals _________.

a. 0.3333
b. 0.0228
c. 0.1111
d. 0.0556

d 26. The probability of obtaining a sum of 2 or 12 equals _________.

a. 0.0228
b. 0.3333
c. 0.0833
d. 0.0556

b 27. The probability of obtaining at least one 3 or one 4 equals _________.

a. 0.3333
b. 0.5556
c. 0.1111
d. 0.0833

d 28. Which of the following are examples of mutually exclusive events?

a. rain and a cloudless sky
b. snow and a temperature of 10° Celsius
c. walking and running at the same time
d. all of the above
e. a and c

Questions 29 - 31 pertain to the following information.

A certain university maintains a colony of male mice for research purposes. The ages of the mice are normally distributed with a mean of 60 days and a standard deviation of 5.2. Assume you randomly sample one mouse from the colony.

c 29. The probability his age will be less than 45 days is _________.

a. 0.9980
b. 0.4980
c. 0.0020
d. 0.0019

a 30. The probability his age will be between 55 and 70 days is _________.

a. 0.8041
b. 0.4980
c. 0.8066
d. 0.1959

b 31. The probability his age will be greater than 68 is _________.

a. 0.4382
b. 0.0618
c. 0.9382
d. 0.0630

Short Answer Questions

1. Define *a posteriori* and *a priori.*
2. Define sampling with replacement and sampling without replacement.
3. Define independent events, mutually exclusive events, and exhaustive events.
4. Why is random sampling important?

True-False Questions

T 1. A random sample results when each possible sample of a given size has an equal chance of being selected.

F 2. When a sampled score is put back in the population before selecting the next score, this process is called sampling without replacement.

F 3. *A priori* and *a posteriori* probability have the same meaning.

T 4. Probability values range from 0 to 1.

T 5. The Addition Rule concerns one of several possible events.

T 6. The Multiplication Rule concerns the joint or successive occurrence of several events.

T 7. If two events are mutually exclusive, they must be dependent.

F 8. If a set of events is exhaustive, they only constitute a part of the possible events.

F 9. For all problems, we must use either the Addition Rule or the Multiplication Rule, but not both.

T 10. When a variable is continuous, $p(A)$ equals the area under the curve corresponding to A divided by the total area under the curve.

T 11. If two events are mutually exclusive and exhaustive, $P + Q = 1$.

F 12. $p(B|A)$ is read probability of B divided by A.

F 13. If sampling is without replacement, the events are independent.

T 14. If an event is certain to occur, its probability of occurrence equals 1.00.

T 15. If an event is certain not to occur, its probability of occurrence equals 0.00.

CHAPTER 9

BINOMIAL DISTRIBUTION

Multiple Choice Questions

d 1. The binomial distribution _________.

a. is a probability distribution
b. gives each possible outcome of *N* trials
c. gives the probability of getting each outcome
d. all of the above
e. b and c

e 2. The requirements for the binomial distribution are _________.

a. a series of *N* trials
b. only two possible outcomes on each trial
c. the outcomes on each trial are mutually exclusive
d. there is independence between trials
e. all of the above
f. a, b and c

a 3. The binomial expansion equals _________.

a. $(P + Q)^N$
b. $P + Q$
c. $(P + Q)^2$
d. 1

b 4. The binomial distribution is symmetrical _________.

a. for all values of *P* and Q
b. only when $P = Q = .50$
c. for $N > 8$
d. for $P > Q$

b 5. As N increases, the binomial distribution _________.

a. becomes skewed
b. becomes more normally distributed
c. is easier to use
d. changes from a discrete to a continuous distribution

For questions 6 - 9 assume the binomial distribution is appropriate.

d 6. If $N = 6$ and $P = 0.50$, the probability of getting exactly 5 P events = ________.

a. 0.1094
b. 0.0156
c. 0.0609
d. 0.0938

a 7. The answer to question 6 derives from evaluating which of the term(s) in the following expansion:

$$P^6 + 6P^5Q + 15P^4Q^2 + 20P^3Q^3 + 15P^2Q^4 + 6PQ^5 + Q^6$$

a. $6P^5Q$
b. $6PQ^5$
c. P^6
d. $P^6 + 6P^5Q$

c 8. If $N = 10$ and $P = 0.30$, the probability of getting at least 8 P events is ________.

a. 0.1493
b. 0.1211
c. 0.0015
d. 0.0014

d 9. If $N = 12$ and $P = 0.60$, the probability of getting exactly 11 P events is ________.

a. 0.0010
b. 0.0003
c. 0.0075
d. 0.0174

a 10. Suppose you gave a multiple-choice exam with 16 questions on it. Each question has 4 alternatives. What is the probability that a student who guesses at random on each of the 16 questions will score 4 or fewer correct answers? Assume that each alternative to each question is equally likely to be chosen.

a. 0.6302
b. 0.7982
c. 0.0383
d. 0.0000

11. A cat lover wants to know if cats have color vision. She teaches her cat to press a green button to obtain a food reward. She then gives the cat a choice between a green and a red button, but only rewards it when it presses the red button. Position of the button is controlled for. The cat is given several practice trials, and then tested 15 times. If the cat cannot distinguish between red and green, what is the probability that it will push the red button at least 12 times out of 15?

a. 0.0139
b. 0.0176
c. 0.0593
d. 0.0037

c 12. A true-false test of 20 questions is given to 10,000 students. If all the students guess on each question, how many students would you expect to get 17 or more questions correct?

a. 0.0013
b. 11
c. 13
d. 0.0011

Short Answer Questions

1. The binomial distribution results when what conditions are met?

2. List three commonly encountered situations where the binomial distribution is applicable and explain how the appropriate conditions are met in each.

3. In an experiment where the binomial distribution is appropriate, six subjects are run. What is the probability of obtaining 6 +'s, if chance alone is at work? Give your answer to <u>six</u> decimal places.

True-False Questions

F 1 The binomial distribution only applies to situations where $P = 0.50$.

F 2 The binomial distribution is always symmetrical.

T 3 The binomial distribution is a discrete distribution.

F 4 The binomial distribution can be used when there are three outcomes on each trial.

T 5 The binomial distribution requires that the P and Q do not change from trial-to-trial.

T 6 $P + Q = 1$

F 7 The binomial distribution only applies to flipping coins and not real life situations.

F 8 For the binomial distribution to be appropriate, P and Q must be equal.

T 9. The binomial distribution requires that P and Q stay the same from trial-to-trial.

CHAPTER 10

INTRODUCTION TO HYPOTHESIS TESTING USING THE SIGN TEST

Multiple Choice Questions

c 1. The nondirectional alternative hypothesis asserts that _________.

a. the results of the experiment were due to chance alone
b. no conclusions can be drawn from the experiment
c. the independent variable has an effect
d. the independent variable has no effect

b 2. The statistic used in the sign test measures _________.

a. the difference between the means of the two groups
b. the direction of the differences between pairs of scores
c. the magnitude of the differences between pairs of scores
d. the difference between the variance of the two groups

a 3. In the sign test, if the null hypothesis is true, then P _________.

a. equals 0.50
b. is greater than 0.50
c. is less than 0.50
d. differs depending on H_1

a 4. An alpha level of 0.05 indicates that _________.

a. if H_0 is true, the probability of falsely rejecting it is limited to 0.05
b. 95% of the time, chance is operating
c. the probability of a Type II error is 0.05
d. the probability of a correct decision is 0.05

d 5. If alpha is changed from 0.05 to 0.01, _________.

a. the probability of a Type II error decreases
b. the probability of a Type I error increases
c. the error probabilities stay the same the probability we will retain a false H_0 increases
d. the probability we will retain a false H_0 increases

e 6. If you reject the null hypothesis, you may be making _________.

a. a Type II error
b. a Type I error
c. a correct decision
d. a and c
e. b and c

d 7. If you retain the null hypothesis, you may be making _________.

a. a Type II error
b. a Type I error
c. a correct decision
d. a and c
e. b and c

f 8. The sign test _________.

a. analyzes the sign of difference scores
b. is used with a repeated measures design
c. uses the binomial distribution
d. evaluates the magnitude of the differences
e. all of the above
f. a, b and c

a 9. In the repeated measures design, _________.

a. differences between paired scores are analyzed
b. the raw scores in each condition are analyzed separately
c. we must use a directional alternative hypothesis
d. all of the above

c 10. The null hypothesis which is appropriate for a directional alternative hypothesis asserts that _________.

a. the independent variable has had no effect
b. chance alone is responsible for the differences between conditions
c. the independent variable does not have an effect in the direction predicted by H_1
d. b and c

b 11. If the alternative hypothesis states that alcohol affects short-term memory, the null hypothesis states _________.

a. alcohol does not decrease short-term memory
b. alcohol has no effect on short-term memory
c. alcohol decreases short-term memory
d. $P \neq Q$

a 12. If alpha equals 0.05 and the probability level of your experiment is 0.04, you would _________.

a. reject the null hypothesis
b. retain the null hypothesis
c. accept the null hypothesis
d. redo the experiment

d 13. Using the sign test, if the null hypothesis is false, then *P* (the probability of a plus) _________.

a. equals 0.50
b. equals alpha
c. equals beta
d. is not equal to 0.50

c 14. In an experiment with a repeated measures design _________.

a. the entire experiment is done twice
b. one group of subjects receives one treatment, the other group receives another treatment
c. the same subjects receive both treatments
d. none of the above

c 15. If alpha is 0.05 and obtained probability level is 0.01, you could be making a _________.

a. Type II error or correct decision
b. Type II error or a Type I error
c. Type I error or a correct decision
d. all of the above

d 16. If we set alpha at 0.05 instead of 0.01 _________.

a. we have a greater risk of a Type I error
b. we have a greater risk of a Type II error
c. we have a lesser risk of a Type II error
d. a and c

b 17. If the alpha level is changed from 0.05 to 0.01, what effect does this have on beta?

a. beta decreases
b. beta increases
c. beta is unaffected
d. cannot be determined

e 18. In stating H_0 and H_1, one must be certain that they are _________.

a. mutually exclusive
b. independent
c. exhaustive
d. a series of *N* trials
e. a and c

c 19. In an experiment involving a nondirectional alternative hypothesis, the obtained result was 7 pluses and 1 minus. To evaluate the null hypothesis, which of the following probabilities would you use?

a. $p(7)$
b. $p(7) + p(8)$
c. $p(0) + p(1) + p(7) + p(8)$
d. $p(1) + p(7)$

a 20. When the results of an experiment are nonsignificant, the proper conclusion(s) is (are) _________.

a. the experiment fails to show a real effect for the independent variable
b. chance alone is at work
c. accept H_0
d. accept H_1
e. the independent variable has no effect
f. a, b, c and e

d 21. It is important to know the possible errors (Type I or Type II) we might make when rejecting or retaining H_0 _________.

a. to minimize these errors when designing the experiment
b. to be aware of the fallacy of "accepting H_0"
c. to maximize the probability of making a correct decision by proper design
d. all of the above
e. a and c

b 22. If $\alpha = 0.05_{1\ \text{tail}}$ and the obtained result has a probability of 0.01 and is in the opposite direction to that predicted by H_1, we conclude by _________.

a. rejecting H_0
b. retaining H_0
c. accepting H_1
d. accepting H_0

c 23. The alpha level _________.

a. is always set at 0.05 or 0.01
b. is set after the data are analyzed
c. is determined by the consequences of making a Type I and Type II error
d. depends on *N*

e 24. When the results are statistically significant, this means _________.

a. the obtained probability is equal to or less than alpha
b. the independent variable has had a large effect
c. we can reject H_0
d. all of the above
e. a and c

In answering questions 25 - 30, refer to the following data.

A psychologist is interested in whether hypnosis affects brain dominance. Twelve college students from the freshmen class are randomly sampled for an experiment. The experiment has two conditions which are given on different days. In condition 1, the students are hypnotized and then given a test which measures the relative dominance of the right and left hemispheres. The higher the score, the more dominant is the right hemisphere. In condition 2, the same students are given the test again, only this time they are not hypnotized but are in their normal state of consciousness. The following scores are obtained.

Student	1	2	3	4	5	6	7	8	9	10	11	12
Condition 1	20	16	22	18	23	30	16	19	14	16	17	25
Condition 2	14	13	17	19	21	22	14	22	12	14	15	22

a 25. The nondirectional alternative hypothesis is _________.

a. hypnosis affects brain dominance
b. hypnosis does not affect brain dominance
c. hypnosis increases right brain dominance
d. hypnosis does not increase right brain dominance

b 26. The null hypothesis appropriate for the nondirectional alternative hypothesis is _________.

a. hypnosis does not increase right brain dominance
b. hypnosis does not affect brain dominance
c. hypnosis does not increase left brain dominance
d. hypnosis affects brain dominance

b 27. The obtained probability = _________.

a. 0.0161
b. 0.0384
c. 0.0192
d. 0.0322

c 28. Using $\alpha = 0.05_{2\text{ tail}}$, your conclusion is _________.

a. accept H_0; hypnosis has no affect on brain dominance
b. retain H_0; we cannot conclude that hypnosis affects brain dominance
c. reject H_0; hypnosis affects brain dominance
d. change H_0

c 29. The population to which these results apply is _________.

a. all students
b. the 12 students in the experiment
c. the freshman class
d. all adults

d 30. The error(s) you may be making by your conclusion in question 28 is (are) _________.

a. a Type I error
b. a Type II error
c. that hypnosis may not affect brain dominance
d. a and c
e. b and c

c 31 Using the sign test, if (1) H_1 is directional, (2) H_0 is false, (3) $\alpha = 0.01$, and (4) N = 12, then the probability of making a Type I error equals _________.

a. 0.0002
b. 0.0010
c. 0
d. 0.0192

d 32 Using the sign test, with $N = 15$ and $\alpha = 0.05_{2\text{-tail}}$, if H_0 is true, the probability of making a type I error equals _________.

a. 0.0042
b. 0
c. 0.05
d. 0.0352
e. none of the above

d 33. If the result of an experiment is statistically significant, this means

a. the result is reliable
b. the result is important
c. if we repeat the experiment, we expect the result to be significant again
d. a and c
e. a, b and c

Short Answer Questions

1. Briefly describe the process involved in hypothesis testing, beginning with H_1 and H_0, and ending with generalization to the population.

2. Define Type I and Type II error. Why is it important to know the possible errors we might make when rejecting or retaining H_0?

3. When is it appropriate to use a directional hypothesis? Discuss.

4. Why is alpha usually set at 0.05 or 0.01?

5. Why do we directly evaluate H_0 rather than H_1?

6. If the obtained probability in an experiment equals 0.1500, then the probability that chance alone is at work equals 0.1500. Is this statement true? Explain.

7. The null hypothesis for a directional H_1 asserts that chance alone is at work or there is a real effect in the direction opposite to that predicted by H_1. This is a correct statement, and yet we reject or retain this H_0 based on assuming chance alone is at work. What about the possibility of a real effect in the opposite direction?

8. What do we mean by "state of reality?"

9. Using the sign test, is the probability of making a Type I error equal to alpha? Why or why not? Illustrate, using an example and appropriate calculations.

10. If a result is statistically significant, this means that the result must be an important one. Is this statement true? Explain.

True-False Questions

T 1. Regardless of whether H_1 is directional or nondirectional, when evaluating H_0 we always assume chance is responsible for the differences in results between conditions.

F 2. Using the sign test, and excluding ties, if H_0 is true the sample data must have half pluses and half minuses.

T 3. If H_0 is true and we reject it, we have made a Type I error.

F 4. If H_0 is false and we reject it, we have made a Type II error.

T 5. If H_0 is false, and we retain it, we have made a Type II error.

F 6. We always evaluate just the specific result obtained in the experiment.

T 7. We always evaluate the tail of the distribution, beginning with the obtained result, rather than just the obtained result itself.

F 8. The alternative hypothesis must be nondirectional.

F 9. We always directly evaluate H_1 when analyzing the data.

F 10. The sign test analyzes both the magnitude and direction of the data.

T 11. The value used for alpha depends on the consequences of making a Type I and Type II error.

F 12. It is always appropriate to use a directional alternative hypothesis.

T 13. H_1 and H_0, taken together, cover the entire continuum with regard to possible effects of the independent variable.

F 14. If results are statistically significant, the independent variable must have had a very large effect.

F 15. It is technically correct to conclude by "accepting" rather than "failing to reject" H_0.

T 16. If the result turns out to be in the direction opposite to a directional H_1, we must conclude by retaining H_0.

T 17. It is permissible to use a directional H_1 when there are good theoretical as well as strong supporting data to justify the predicted direction.

F 18. It is always appropriate to use a directional H_1.

T 19. It is impossible to prove with certainty the truth of H_1 when using sample data.

F 20. If H_0 is validly rejected, H_1 must be true.

T 21. The sign test is used with the replicated measures design.

T 22. If alpha is made more stringent, beta increases.

T 23. If H_0 is true, beta equals 0.00.

CHAPTER 11

POWER

Multiple Choice Questions

a 1. With alpha and the effect of the independent variable held constant, as *N* increases _________.

a. power increases
b. the probability of a Type I error increases
c. the probability of a Type II error increases
d. power decreases

b 2. With alpha and *N* held constant, as the effect of the independent variable increases _________.

a. the probability of rejecting H_0 increases
b. power increases
c. the probability of rejecting H_0 remains the same
d. the probability of making a Type II error decreases
e. a, b, and d
f. a and b

c 3. With the effect of the independent variable and *N* held constant, as α gets more stringent _________.

a. power increases
b. power stays the same
c. power decreases
d. beta decreases

b 4. The advantage of a powerful experiment is that _________.

a. the probability of a Type I error is reduced.
b. you are more likely to detect the real effects of the independent variable, if there are any.
c. as power increases, alpha increases.
d. as power increases, *N* increases

a 5. If H_0 is in reality false and it is legitimate to use a directional H_1, which of the following will yield a more powerful test?

a. one-tailed alternative hypothesis
b. two-tailed alternative hypothesis
c. one-tailed or two-tailed alternative hypothesis will yield the same power
d. type of alternative hypothesis has no effect on power

c 6. If H_0 is true and the probability of making a Type I error is 0.05, then the probability of making a correct decision is ________.

a. power
b. 0.05
c. 0.95
d. need more information

b 7. In an experiment in which H_1 is nondirectional, and the state of reality is such that the probability of a plus = 0.50, the probability of making a Type II error is ________.

a. 1 – alpha
b. 0
c. 1
d. need more information

b 8. Maximizing the power of an experiment ________.

a. minimizes alpha
b. minimizes beta
c. increases the probability of rejecting H_0 when H_0 is true
d. increases the probability of making a Type II error

c 9. If H_0 is true, then the probability of rejecting H_0 is limited by ________.

a. Power
b. 1 – power
c. alpha
d. beta

a 10 Which of the following values of P represents the largest effect?

a. $P_{real} = 0.20$
b. $P_{real} = 0.70$
c. $P_{real} = 0.75$
d. $P_{null} = 0.50$

b 11. If $N = 4$, $P_{real} = 0.80$ in the direction predicted, and $\alpha = 0.05_{1\ tail}$, using the sign test, the power is ________.

a. 0.9375
b. 0.0000
c. 1.0000
d. 0.0625

c 12 If H_1 is nondirectional and the size of the effect of the independent variable decreases, the probability of making a Type I error _________.

a. decreases
b. increases
c. equals zero
d. need more information

a 13. With other factors held constant, as the effect of the independent variable decreases, power will _________ and the probability of a Type II error will _________.

a. decrease, increase
b. decrease, decrease
c. increase, decrease
d. increase, increase

d 14. The power of an experiment is affected by _________.

a. the alpha level
b. the sample size
c. the size of effect of the independent variable
d. all of the above

d. 15. If the null hypothesis is false, the probability of making a correct decision is given by _________.

a. alpha
b. beta
c. 1 – alpha
d. power

c. 16. If the power of an experiment is 0.7496, the probability of making a Type II error is _________.

a. 0.2498
b. 0.05
c. 0.2504
d. cannot tell without more information

b. 17 You can only compute power when ________.

a. alpha > 0.05
b. H_1 is given
c. Beta > 0.05
d. 1 – power = 0.05

b 18. Power equals ________

a. alpha + beta
b. 1 – beta
c. 1 – alpha
d. alpha – beta

c 19. You are considering testing a new drug that is supposed to facilitate learning in mentally retarded children. Because there is relatively little known about the drug, you plan to use a nondirectional alternative hypothesis. Since your resources are limited, you can test only 15 subjects. The subjects will be run in a repeated measures design and the data will be analyzed with the sign test, using $\alpha = 0.05_{2\text{ tail}}$. If the drug has a moderate effect on learning such that $P_{real} = 0.70$, what is the probability you will detect the effect when doing your experiment.

a. 0.2968
b. 0.0176
c. 0.2969
d. 0.0352

b. 20. In question 19, what is the probability of a Type II error?

a. 0.7032
b. 0.7031
c. 0.9824
d. 0.9648

Short Answer Questions

b. Give three definitions of power.

c. Define P_{real} and P_{null}.

d. List three variables (not including beta) that affect power and state how increases in the variables affect power.

e. Is it correct to conclude by "accepting" H_0 when the results of an experiment are not significant? Explain.

True-False Questions

T 1. If H_0 is false, as the power of the experiment increases, the probability of rejecting H_0 increases.

F 2. If H_0 is true, as the power of the experiment increases, the probability of rejecting H_0 increases.

F 3. Increasing *N* affects the magnitude of the effect of the independent variable.

T 4. Power is a measure of the sensitivity of an experiment to detect the real effects of the independent variable, if there are any.

T 5. Using sample data, it is impossible to prove with certainty that H_0 is true.

F 6. In general, the sum of alpha and beta should equal 1.

T 7. Power and beta are inversely related.

F 8. Increasing *N* increases the probability of a Type II error.

T 9. Other factors held constant, a one-tailed test is more powerful than a two-tailed test.

T 10. Power is the probability of rejecting H_0 if it is false.

T 11. High power is desirable in an experiment.

F 12. Power varies from −1 to +1.

T 13. A power analysis is useful when the results of an experiment fail to reach significance.

F 14. Decreasing beta will generally cause α to increase.

F 15. Alpha + beta = 1.

CHAPTER 12

Sampling Distributions, Sampling Distribution of the Mean The Normal Deviate (*z*) Test

Multiple Choice Questions

d 1. The sampling distribution of a statistic _________.

a. gives all the values a statistic can take
b. gives the probability of getting each value of a statistic under the assumption it had resulted due to chance alone
c. is a probability distribution
d. all of the above
e. a and b

d 2. Data analysis involving statistical inference basically involves _________.

a. determining the standard deviation of the scores
b. calculating the appropriate statistic
c. evaluating the statistic based on its sampling distribution
d. b and c

f 3. Sampling distributions can be obtained empirically by _________.

a. determining all possible samples of size *N* that can be formed from the Null Hypothesis Population
b. calculating the statistic for each of the samples
c. calculating the probability of getting each value of the statistic, if chance alone is operating
d. selecting several samples from all possible samples and calculating the statistic for those samples
e. all of the above
f. a, b and c
g. b, c and d

a 4. The Null Hypothesis Population is an actual or theoretical set of population scores that would result if _________.

   a. the experiment were done on the entire population and the independent variable had no effect
   b. the experiment were done on the sample and the independent variable had no effect
   c. the experiment were done on the entire population and the independent variable had a real effect
   d. the subjects in the population believed the null hypothesis was true

e 5. A sampling distribution gives all the values a statistic can take, along with _________.

   a. the probability of getting each value if sampling is random from the Null Hypothesis Population
   b. the probability of getting each value under the assumption that it had resulted due to chance alone
   c. the number of samples in the distribution
   d. all of the above
   e. a and b

a 6. Which of the following are true?

   a. $\mu_{\overline{X}}$ is the mean of the sampling distribution of the mean
   b. $\sigma_{\overline{X}}$ is the standard deviation of the raw scores
   c. a and b
   d. none of the above

f 7. The sampling distribution of the mean gives _________.

   a. all the values the sample mean can take
   b. the probability of getting each mean value if sampling is random from the *H*0 population
   c. all the values the sample standard deviation can take
   d. the probability of getting each standard deviation value if sampling is random from the *H*0 population
   e. all of the above
   f. a and b
   g. c and d

c 8. A normally distributed set of population scores has a mean of 65 and a standard deviation of 10.2. The mean, of the sampling distribution of the mean, for samples of size 48 equals _________.

a. 1.35
b. 60
c. 65
d. none of the above

b 9. For the population and sample size given in question 8, the standard error of the mean equals _________.

a. 4.8
b. 1.47
c. 0.21
d. 65

a 10. The mean attention span for adults in a certain village is 15 minutes with a standard deviation of 6.4. The mean of all possible samples of size 30, taken from that population equals _________.

a. 15
b. 0.50
c. 30
d. 2.34

d 11. Using the data given in question 10, $\sigma_{\overline{X}}$ = _________.

a. 3.0
b. 6.4
c. 0.21
d. 1.17

b 12. Using the population of question 10, what is the probability of randomly selecting a sample of 30 scores which has a mean attention span equal to or greater than 17 minutes?

a. 0.3783
b. 0.0436
c. 0.0446
d. 0.4564

a 13. As sample size increases, $\sigma_{\overline{X}}$ _________.

a. decreases
b. increases
c. stays the same
d. approaches σ

b 14. If the variability of the raw score population increases and *N* is held constant, $\sigma_{\overline{X}}$ _________.

a. decreases
b. increases
c. stays the same
d. need more information

c 15. The normal deviate test is used with _________.

a. a replicated measures design
b. an independent groups design
c. a single sample design
d. a multi-group design

e 16. The sampling distribution of the mean _________.

a. is always normally distributed
b. is normally distributed if the population raw scores are normally distributed
c. is considered normally distributed if $N > 300$
d. all of the above
e. b and c

d 17. We can reject H_0 if _________.

a. $z_{obt} = z_{crit}$
b. $z_{obt} \geq z_{crit}$
c. $z_{obt} \leq z_{crit}$
d. $|z_{obt}| \geq |z_{crit}|$

a 18. For the z test, the critical region for rejection of H_0 _________.

a. is determined only by α
b. is determined by α and N
c. allows us to accept the null hypothesis
d. depends on N

d 19. To use the *z* test, _________.

a. μ and σ must be specified
b. the sampling distribution of $\overline{X}$ should be normal
c. the population of raw scores must be normally distributed
d. a and b
e. all of the above

f 20. Which of the following apply to the sampling distribution of the mean?

a. $\mu_{\overline{X}} = \mu$
b. $\sigma_{\overline{X}} = \sigma/\sqrt{N}$
c. the variability of the distribution depends on *N*
d. the shape of the distribution is always normal
e. all of the above
f. a, b and c

c 21. If we take all possible samples from a normally distributed population, which of the following sample sizes will yield the smallest variation in the means of the samples?

a. 1
b. 85
c. 120
d. 5
e. 15

For questions 22 - 24, refer to the following information.

An English teacher has been teaching a sixth grade composition class for many years. He has the feeling that over the past several years, the writing ability of students has changed. A national test of proficiency in composition was administered 5 years ago. The resulting distribution of scores was normally shaped, had a mean of 85 and a standard deviation of 10.9. In order to test his feeling, he gives his present class of 43 students the same proficiency test. The resulting mean is 80 and the standard deviation is 8.7.

c 22. The obtained value of the appropriate statistic for testing H_0 is _________.

a. $z_{obt} = -0.46$
b. $z_{obt} = +3.01$
c. $z_{obt} = -3.01$
d. $z_{obt} = -0.45$

b 23. Using $\alpha = .05_{2\ tail}$, the appropriate critical value is _________.

a. $z_{crit} = -1.645$
b. $z_{crit} = \pm 1.96$
c. $z_{crit} = -1.96$
d. $z_{crit} = \pm 1.645$

a 24. What is your conclusion, using $\alpha = .05_{2\ tail}$?

a. reject H_0; the present class appears deficient in composition writing
b. retain H_0; the present class is not deficient in composition writing
c. accept H_0; the present class is not deficient in composition writing
d. reject H_0; the present class is not deficient in composition writing

e 25. Power increases with ________.

a. increasing N
b. increasing magnitude of the effect of the independent variable
c. increasing α level
d. the magnitude of the difference between μ_{real} and μ_{null}
e. all of the above
f. a, b and c

For questions 26-32, refer to the following material.

A set of sample scores from an experiment has an N = 28 and a mean = 52. H_1 is directional, predicting an effect of the independent variable which decreases the magnitude of the dependent variable. H_0 asserts the sample is a random sample from a population of scores where μ = 55 and σ = 12. α = 0.05 1 tail

a 26. z_{obt} = ________.

a. −1.322
b. −0.250
c. −7.000
d. −0.132

c 27. z_{crit} = ________.

a. +1.96
b. −1.96
c. −1.645
d. +1.645

b 28. What is the correct conclusion regarding H_0?

a. reject H_0; the independent variable has a real effect
b. retain H_0; we cannot conclude that the independent variable has a real effect
c. accept H_0; the independent variable has no effect
d. reject H_0; the independent variable has no effect

d 29. The power of the experiment to detect a real effect such that μ_{real} = 53 is ________.

a. 0.3541
b. 0.7764
c. 0.7600
d. 0.2236

a 30. The probability of making a Type II error is _________.

a. 0.7764
b. 0.2400
c. 0.2236
d. 0.6459

c 31. If *N* is increased to 90, power = _________ to detect a real effect such that μ_{real} = 53.

a. 0.8524
b. 0.9103
c. 0.4761
d. 0.5142

b 32. How high must N be to be able to detect a μ_{real} = 53 with a power of 0.8000?

a. 158
b. 222
c. 173
d. 248

Short Answer Questions

1. Define the sampling distribution of a statistic.
2. Why is it important to know the sampling distribution of a statistic, if we are to use the statistic for inference?
3. Define the critical region and the critical values of a statistic.
4. What are the assumptions underlying the *z* test?
5. What are the characteristics of the sampling distribution of the mean?
6. Explain the process of generating sampling distributions using the empirical approach.
7. Explain why $\sigma_{\overline{X}}$ should vary directly with σ and inversely with *N*.
8. Define μ_{null} and μ_{real}.

True-False Questions

T 1. Generally speaking, if the sampling distribution of a statistic is indeterminate (impossible to determine), the statistic cannot be used for inference.

F 2. The sampling distribution of the mean is always normally distributed.

F 3. The sampling distribution of z is always normally distributed.

F 4. The sampling distribution of z varies with the size of the sample.

T 5. The sampling distribution of the mean varies with the size of the sample.

T 6. The symbol for the mean of the sampling distribution of the mean is $\mu_{\overline{X}}$.

T 7. The symbol for the standard error of the mean is $\sigma_{\overline{X}}$.

T 8. The normal deviate test uses the mean of the sample as a basic statistic.

T 9. The sampling distribution of z must be normally distributed to use the z test.

T 10. To use the z test, μ and σ must be specified.

F 11. The z test does not depend on the shape of the sampling distribution of $\overline{X}$.

F 12. As N increases, the variability of the sampling distribution of the mean increases.

T 13. $\mu_{\overline{X}} = \mu$, regardless of the shape of the sampling distribution of the mean.

F 14. The critical region for rejection of H_0 is the area under the curve that contains all the values of the statistic that fail to allow rejection of H_0.

T 15. The critical value of a statistic is the value of the statistic that bounds the critical region for rejection of H_0.

T 16. The sampling distribution of the mean is made up of mean scores.

F 17. Using the sample standard deviation as an estimate for the population standard deviation is an example of interval estimation.

T 18. Power is the sensitivity of the experiment to detect a real effect of the independent variable, if there is one.

T 19. Power + Beta = 1.

F 20. In general, Alpha + Beta = 1.

T 21. If H_0 is false, a high level of power increases the probability we will reject it.

F 22. Increasing *N* increases the real effect of the independent variable.

T 23. High power is desirable in an experiment.

T 24. Alpha and Beta are inversely related.

F 25. Power and Beta are directly related.

CHAPTER 13

STUDENT'S *t* TEST FOR SINGLE SAMPLES

Multiple Choice Questions

c 1. In an independent groups experiment, if we must estimate the population standard deviation to determine the significance of the sample results, the appropriate inference test is the _________.

a. sign test
b. *z* test
c. *t* test
d. none of the above

c 2. For a given *N*, the interval that bounds the population mean at the 99% confidence level is _________ that which bounds the population mean at the 95% confidence level.

a. equal to
b. greater than
c. less than
d. can't be determined without knowing $s_{\overline{X}}$

b 3. The mean of the *t* distribution equals _________.

a. the mean of the population of raw scores
b. 0
c. 1
d. σ

a 4. $|t_{crit}|$ for any alpha level is _________ $|z_{crit}|$ for *N* less than infinity.

a. greater than
b. the same as
c. less than
d. none of the above

d 5. Which of the following represents a sampling distribution?

a. the binomial distribution
b. the *z* distribution
c. the *t* distribution
d. all of the above
e. b and c

b 6. When using the t test, we reject H_0 _________.

a. if $t_{obt} \le t_{crit}$
b. if $| t_{obt} | \ge | t_{crit} |$
c. if $| t_{obt} | \le | t_{crit} |$
d. if $t_{obt} \ge t_{crit}$

d 7. The sampling distribution of *t* depends on _________.

a. μ
b. σ
c. s
d. df
e. α
f. all of the above

b 8. In a *t* test, when the size of the sample is increased, the confidence interval _________.

a. increases
b. decreases
c. stays the same
d. changes shape
e. a and d

c 9. The 95% confidence interval arrived at from a particular experiment is 72-79. This means that _________.

a. the probability is 0.95 that μ falls between 72-79
b. the probability is 0.95 that the interval 72-79 contains $\overline{X}$
c. the probability is 0.95 that the interval 72-79 contains μ
d. a and c

c 10. Which of the characteristics below distinguishes the *t* statistic from the *z* statistic?

a. the proportion of area beyond a particular positive *t* value is equal to the proportion of area below the corresponding negative *t*
b. the *z* distribution has a mean of zero while the *t* distribution does not
c. In the *t* distribution the area under the curve beyond a value of ±1.96 is greater than that of the normal curve
d. all of the above

b 11. As the df increases, the *t* distribution _________.

a. gets more symmetrical
b. approaches the normal distribution
c. stays the same
d. becomes more skewed

d 12. With which statistical test do we determine the probability of getting the obtained results or those more extreme assuming the differences in results were due to chance alone?

a. sign test
b. *z* test
c. *t* test
d. all of the above

a 13. In a correlated groups experiment, if we must estimate the population standard deviation to determine the significance of the sample results, the appropriate statistical test is _________.

a. *t* test
b. sign test
c. *z* test
d. none of the above

a 14. As the degrees of freedom increase, the correspondence between the *t* and *z* distributions _________.

a. increases
b. decreases
c. remains the same
d. cannot be determined

e 15. The *t* test differs from the *z* test in that _________.

a. with the t test we estimate σ
b. with the *t* test we estimate μ
c. the *z* distribution is a family of curves
d. the *t* distribution is a family of curves
e. a and d

c 16. $s_{\overline{X}}$ is an estimate of _________.

a. μ
b. σ
c. $\sigma_{\overline{X}}$
d. s

d 17. We lose one degree of freedom in calculating _________.

a. s
b. $\overline{X}$
c. t_{obt} (single sample)
d. a and c

b 18. The degrees of freedom for the *t* test for single samples are _________.

a. N
b. $N - 1$
c. $N - 2$
d. depends on alpha

a 19. The confidence interval for the population mean is _________.

a. a range of values which probably contains the population mean
b. a range of values which contains the population mean
c. the same from sample-to-sample
d. a and c

f 20. In a correlative study, _________.

a. a value of $r \neq 0$ in the sample, means that there is a nonzero correlation in the population
b. a nondirectional alternative hypothesis states that $\rho \neq 0$
c. the null hypothesis for a nondirectional alternative hypothesis states that $\rho = 0$
d. a nondirectional alternative hypothesis states that $r = 0$
e. all of the above
f. b and c

c 21. The df associated with evaluating the significance of r_{obt} are _________.

a. N
b. $N - 1$
c. $N - 2$
d. need more information

Use the following information for questions 22 - 25.

A researcher believes that women today weigh less than in previous years. To investigate this belief, he randomly samples 41 adult women and records their weights. The scores have a mean of 111 lbs. and a standard deviation of 12.4. A local census taken several years ago shows the mean weight of adult women was 115 lbs.

a 22. The obtained value of the appropriate statistic for testing H_0 is _________.

a. $t_{obt} = -2.07$
b. $t_{obt} = +2.07$
c. $t_{obt} = -0.32$
d. $t_{obt} = +0.32$

b 23. The df for determining t_{crit} = _________.

a. 41
b. 40
c. 39
d. need more information

b 24. Using $\alpha = 0.01_{1\ \text{tail}}$, the appropriate critical value is _________.

a. −1.684
b. −2.423
c. ±1.684
d. ±2.423

d 25. What do you conclude, using $\alpha = 0.01_{1\ \text{tail}}$?

a. accept H_1
b. accept H_0
c. reject H_0
d. retain H_0
e. a and c

b 26. Use the data presented in Chapter 7, question 25. In that question, $r_{obt} = -0.70$ and $N = 6$. Using $\alpha = 0.05_{2\ \text{tail}}$, is this a significant value for r_{obt}?

a. No, df = 5, $r_{crit} = \pm 0.7545$
b. No, df = 4, $r_{crit} = \pm 0.8114$
c. No, df = 4, $r_{crit} = -0.8114$
d. No, df = 4, $r_{crit} = +0.8114$

Short Answer Questions

1. Define confidence interval and confidence limits.
2. Describe the characteristics of the sampling distribution of *t*.
3. Define degrees of freedom.
4. What are the assumptions underlying the *t* test for single samples.
5. Which test, *z* or *t*, has higher power? Explain why.

True-False Questions

F 1. There are two values for t_{crit} when H_1 is directional.

T 2. As the degrees of freedom increase, the *t* distribution becomes more like the *z* distribution.

T 3. The *t* distribution is a family of curves that vary with the degrees of freedom.

F 4. If we have to estimate σ, we should use the *z* test.

T 5. The degrees of freedom equal $N - 1$ for the *t* test for single samples.

T 6. To test the significance of r_{obt}, the df = $N - 2$.

F 7. The *t* test is more sensitive than the *z* test.

F 8. t_{crit} must always be positive.

F 9. The *t* test requires that the sampling distribution of *t* be normally distributed.

T 10. If $N < 30$, to use the *t* test, the population of raw scores should be normally distributed.

T 11. Generally speaking, the more confidence we have that the interval contains the population mean, the larger is the interval.

T 12. $\overline{X}_{obt} \pm s_{\overline{X}} t_{crit}$ determines the confidence interval for the population mean.

F 13. In general, if $r = 0$, then $\rho = 0$.

F 14. In general, if $r \neq 0$, then ρ must not equal 0.

F 15. If $r > 0.50$, then there must be a nonzero correlation in the population.

T 16. If $| r_{obt} | > | r_{crit} |$, we reject the assumption that $\rho = 0$.

CHAPTER 14

STUDENT'S *t* TEST FOR CORRELATED AND INDEPENDENT GROUPS

Multiple Choice Questions

d 1. For which of these tests do you need to know the sampling distribution of the relevant statistic in order to use the statistic for hypothesis testing?

a. *z* test
b. *t* test
c. sign test
d. all of the above

d 2. The power of the *t* test increases with _________.

a. increases in *N*
b. increases in the effect of the independent variable
c. decreases in the sample variance(s)
d. all of the above
e. a and b

b 3. In an experiment using the independent groups design, there are 10 subjects in one group and 12 subjects in the other group. The sampling distribution of t that is appropriate for that experiment is identical to the *t* distribution that is appropriate for a single sample design with _________ subjects.

a. 22
b. 21
c. 20
d. 11

e 4. Which of the following are assumptions underlying the use of the *t* test for independent groups?

a. the variance of each population is known
b. the sampling distribution of $\overline{X}_1 - \overline{X}_2$ must be normal
c. the samples are drawn from populations having equal variances
d. all of the above
e. b and c

e 5. If the homogeneity of variance assumption is violated in an experiment using the *t* test for independent groups, this means _________.

a. the populations from which the samples were drawn have different variances
b. the power of the *t* test will be reduced
c. t the test can still be used, if the violation is a moderate one
d. the t test should not be used
e. a and c
f. a, b and c

e 6. A correlated groups design is more sensitive than an independent groups design if _________.

a. there are large inter-subject differences
b. there are small inter-subject differences
c. the experimental treatment effect is strong
d. there is a high correlation between paired scores
e. a and e

b 7. The null hypothesis for a nondirectional H_1 using the *t* test for correlated groups asserts that _________.

a. $\mu_1 - \mu_2 = 0$
b. $\mu_D = 0$
c. $\mu_{\overline{D}} = 0$
d. $D - \mu_{\overline{D}} = 0$
e. none of the above

a 8. Assuming large between subject variability, which of the following tests is usually the most sensitive (*N* held constant)?

a. *t* test for correlated groups
b. sign test
c. *t* test for independent groups
d. they are all equal in sensitivity

d 9. If the homogeneity of variance assumption is violated in an independent groups *t* test, this means _________.

a. the populations from which the samples were drawn have different standard deviations
b. you should use the sign test
c. the sample sizes should be equal and N greater than 30 to use the t test
d. a and c
e. all of the above

d 10. One employs a correlated groups design _________.

a. to eliminate random error
b. to simplify calculations
c. for prediction
d. to reduce the effects of individual differences among subjects

c 11. In employing a correlated groups design, one possible drawback is _________.

a. the increased number of statistical computations
b. random errors are likely to be greater
c. reduction in the degrees of freedom
d. none of the above

d 12. Having just made what you feel is to be a Type II error, using an independent groups design and a t test analysis, which of the following might you do in the next experiment to reduce the probability of a Type II error?

a. increase N
b. change to a correlated groups design
c. try to reduce the variance by better experimental control
d. all of the above
e. a and b

d 13. The mean of the sampling distribution of $\overline{X}_1 - \overline{X}_2 =$ _________.

a. μ
b. 0
c. 1
d. $\mu_1 - \mu_2$

c 14. The z test for independent groups is seldom used because _________.

a. it lacks sensitivity
b. it is too complicated
c. we seldom know the population variances
d. the sampling distribution of z under H_0 is unknown

e 15. Which of the following increase(s) the power of the t test?

a. increasing N
b. increasing the sample variance(s)
c. increasing the effect of the independent variable
d. all of the above
e. a and c

b 16. In a *t* test for two independent samples, the unbiased estimate of the population variance is

a. $$\frac{(\overline{X}_1 - \overline{X}_2) - \mu_{\overline{X}_1 - \overline{X}_2}}{\sqrt{\left(\frac{SS_1 + SS_2}{n_1 + n_2 - 2}\right)\left(\frac{1}{n_1} + \frac{1}{n_2}\right)}}$$

b. $$\frac{SS_1 + SS_2}{n_1 + n_2 - 2}$$

c. $$\left(\frac{SS_1 + SS_2}{n_1 + n_2 - 2}\right)\left(\frac{1}{n_1} + \frac{1}{n_2}\right)$$

d. $$\sqrt{\left(\frac{SS_1 + SS_2}{n_1 + n_2 - 2}\right)\left(\frac{1}{n_1} + \frac{1}{n_2}\right)}$$

d 17. Which of the following is (are) major advantage(s) of a two condition experiment over a single sample design?

a. A lack of dependence on population values which may be inappropriate
b. no need to know any parameters of the raw score population
c. creates ability to control for other variables which may affect the results
d. all of the above
e. a and b

b 18. Student's *t* test for correlated groups really reduces to _________.

a. the sign test
b. Student's *t* test for single samples using difference scores
c. Students *t* test for independent groups
d. none of the above

a 19. Student's *t* test for correlated groups is _________.

a. more powerful than the sign test because it uses both the magnitude and direction of the scores
b. less powerful than the sign test because it uses only the magnitude of the scores
c. impractical because we need to know σ
d. generally less powerful than Student's *t* test for independent groups
e. a and c

d 20. The *t* test for correlated groups requires that _________.

a. the sampling distribution of $\overline{X}$ is normally distributed
b. $N \geq 30$
c. the population raw scores are normally distributed
d. the sampling distribution of $\overline{D}$ is normally is normally distributed
e. b, c and d

d 21. Using the *t* test for independent groups, a directional alternative hypothesis predicts _________.

a. $\mu_1 > \mu_2$
b. $\mu_1 = \mu_2$
c. $\mu_1 < \mu_2$
d. a or c, depending on the direction
e. all of the above

a 22. $\mu_{\overline{X}_1 - \overline{X}_2}$ equals _________.

a. $\mu_1 - \mu_2$
b. 0
c. 1
d. it depends on the sample

b 23. In the *t* test for independent groups, _________.

a. we estimate $\mu_1 - \mu_2$
b. we estimate σ^2
c. we estimate $\overline{X}_1 - \overline{X}_2$
d. df = $N - 1$

f 24. If a test is a robust test,

a. it is sensitive to its underlying mathematical assumptions
b. it doesn't estimate any population parameters
c. it is insensitive to its underlying mathematical assumptions
d. it often may be used despite violations of its underlying mathematical assumptions
e. b, c and d
f. c and d

In answering questions 25 - 28 refer to the following data.

A professor of women's studies is interested in determining if stress affects the menstrual cycle. Ten women are randomly sampled for an experiment and randomly divided into two groups. One of the groups

is subjected to high stress for two months while the other lives in a relatively stress-free environment. The professor measures the menstrual cycle (in days) of each woman during the second month. The following data are obtained.

High stress	**20**	**23**	**18**	**19**	**22**
Relatively stress free	**26**	**31**	**25**	**26**	**30**

a 25. The obtained value of the appropriate statistic is ________.

a. $t_{obt} = -4.73$
b. $t_{obt} = -4.71$
c. $t_{obt} = -3.05$
d. $t_{obt} = -0.47$

c 26. The df for determining t_{crit} are ________.

a. 4
b. 9
c. 8
d. 3

d 27. Using $\alpha = .05_{2 \text{ tail}}$, t_{crit} = ________.

a. +2.262
b. +2.306
c. ±2.262
d. ±2.306

d 28. Using $\alpha = .05_{2 \text{ tail}}$, your conclusion is ________.

a. accept H_0; stress does not affect the menstrual cycle
b. retain H_0; we cannot conclude that stress affects the menstrual cycle
d. retain H_0; stress affects the menstrual cycle
d. reject H_0; stress affects the menstrual cycle

b 29. Estimate the size of the effect. $\hat{\omega}^2$ = ________.

a. 0.8102
b. 0.6810
c. 0.4322
d. 0.5776

In answering questions 30 - 33, refer to the following experiment.

A health educator wants to evaluate the effect of a dental film on the frequency with which children brush their teeth. A random selection of

8 children are used for the experiment. First, a baseline of the number of times the children brush their teeth over a month's period is established. Next, the children are shown the dental film and again the number of teeth brushings are recorded for a month. The following data are recorded.

Subject	**1**	**2**	**3**	**4**	**5**	**6**	**7**	**8**
After film	**28**	**29**	**25**	**30**	**25**	**27**	**28**	**24**
Baseline	**25**	**28**	**22**	**30**	**26**	**24**	**25**	**22**

a 30. The obtained value of the appropriate statistic is ________.

a. 3.13
b. 3.14
c. 3.58
d. 3.57

c 31. The df for determining t_{crit} equal ________.

a. 8
b. 16
c. 7
d. 14

b 32. Using $\alpha = .05_{2\ tail}$, t_{crit} = ________.

a. +2.365
b. ±2.365
c. ±2.145
d. +2.365

b 33. Using $\alpha = 0.05_{2\ tail}$, what do you conclude?

a. retain H_0; the film has no effect on the frequency of tooth brushing
b. reject H_0; the film affects the frequency of tooth brushing
c. accept H_0; the film has no effect on the frequency of tooth brushing
e. reject H_0; chance alone is a reasonable explanation of the data

e 34. In the *t* test for independent groups, the unbiased estimate of the population variance 2 is ________.

a. s_1^2 alone
b. s_2^2 alone
c. a weighted average of s_1^2 and s_2^2
d. $(SS_1 + SS_2)/(n_1 + n_2 - 2)$
e. c and d

Short Answer Questions

1. You are comparing two methods of psychotherapy, Method *A* and Method *B*. You have randomly assigned 10 subjects to method *A* and 10 other subjects to Method *B*. The dependent variable is the number of weeks in therapy to achieve a cure. The variance of Method *A* scores turns out to be somewhat greater than Method *B* scores. What inference test would you use? Explain.

2. You are interested in whether chewing nicotine gum reduces smoking. You record the number of cigarettes smoked daily by 15 subjects under normal conditions. One week later, you have them chew nicotine gum for two weeks and record the number of cigarettes smoked daily during the two weeks. The data turns out to be very skewed. What inference test would you use? Explain.

3. Compare and contrast the independent groups design with the correlated groups design.

4. What are the assumptions underlying the *t* test for independent groups.

5. How does the variability of the sample data affect the power of the *t* test. Explain, using the appropriate equations.

6. What are the variables that affect the power of the t test? How does each variable affect power, when its value increases? .

7. In addition to determining whether a result is significant, it may be important to know the size of the effect. Is this statement correct? Explain.

True-False Questions

T 1. The *t* test for correlated groups is just like the *t* test for single samples except that it analyzes difference scores.

T 2. The power of the *t* test increases with increases in the effect of the independent variable.

F 3. The power of the *t* test increases with increases in sample variability.

F 4. In a correlated groups design with a directional H_1, if H_0 is correct, the sample set of difference scores must be a random sample from a population of difference scores with $\mu_D = 0$.

T 5. In a correlated groups design, the reasonableness of the null hypothesis is usually tested by assuming the sample set of difference scores is a random sample from a population of difference scores with $\mu_D = 0$.

T 6. In an independent groups design, if the independent variable has a real effect, $\mu_1 \neq \mu_2$.

F 7. If the homogeneity of variance assumption is not met, it is invalid to use the *t* test for independent groups.

F 8. If the correlation is zero between paired scores, the *t* test for correlated groups is more powerful than the t test for independent groups.

T 9. In the t test for correlated groups, a directional H_1 may predict $\mu_D > 0$.

F 10. The sampling distribution of *t* is different for single samples than for correlated groups.

T 11. The *t* test for correlated groups uses both the magnitude and direction of the difference scores.

T 12. Ties are included in the analysis when using the *t* test for correlated groups.

T 13. The *z* test for independent groups is seldom used because σ^2 is unknown.

T 14. The estimate of σ^2 used in the t test for independent groups is an estimated based on the variances of both samples.

F 15. Homogeneity of variance means that $\mu_1 = \mu_2$.

T 16. $\mu_{\overline{X}1-\overline{X}2} = \mu_1 - \mu_2$

T 17. A robust test is relatively insensitive to violations of its underlying mathematical assumptions.

T 18. The *t* test for independent groups is a robust test.

F 19. In an independent groups experiment, if the independent variable has no effect, $\mu_1 \neq \mu_2$.

T 20. If the independent variable has a real effect, the *t* test for independent groups assumes $\sigma_1^2 = \sigma_2^2$.

CHAPTER 15

INTRODUCTION TO THE ANALYSIS OF VARIANCE

Multiple Choice Questions

e 1. The null hypothesis in the one-way ANOVA asserts that _________.

a. the within groups variance estimate is an estimate of the population variance
b. $\mu_1 = \mu_2 = \mu_3 = \mu_k$
c. the between group variance estimate and the within group variance estimate are both estimates of the same population variance
d. the within group sum of squares is equal to the between group sum of squares
e. b and c

d 2. Which of the following increase(s) as the difference between the group means increases?

a. s_B^2
b. F_{obt}
c. t_{obt}
d. all of the above

d 3. Which of the following is (are) assumption(s) underlying the use of the *F* test?

a. the raw score populations are normally distributed
b. the variances of the raw score populations are the same
c. the mean of the populations differ
d. a and b
e. all of the above

b 4. The parameter being estimated in the analysis of variance is the _________.

a. sample mean
b. variance of the H_0 populations
c. sample variance
d. mean of the H_0 populations
e. F_{obt}

d 5. If its assumptions are met, the analysis of variance technique is appropriate when _________.

a. two or more factors are varied
b. several levels of a single independent variable are compared
c. three or more groups are involved
d. all of the above

a 6. As the differences between the group means increases, _________.

a. s_B^2 increases
b. F_{obt} decreases
c. t_{obt} decreases
d. all of the above
e. none of the above

b 7. If $SS_T = 20$ and $SS_B = 14$, $SS_W =$ _________.

a. 34
b. 6
c. –6
d. need more information

a 8. The F ratio increases as _________.

a. the variability between means increases relative to the variability within groups
b. the variability between means decreases relative to the variability within groups
c. the total variability increases
d. the total variability decreases
e. the variability within groups remains the same

g 9. Which of the following is (are) true about the F distribution?

a. it has no negative values
b. it is positively skewed
c. there are a family of *F* curves uniquely determined by df(numerator) and df(denominator)
d. the mean of the *F* distribution equals 0
e. all of the above
f. a and b
g. a, b and c

b 10. A major limitation of a two group design is that _________.

a. we can't run enough subjects
b. very often, two groups are insufficient for a clear interpretation
c. the population parameters may not be applicable
d. the means between groups may not differ

b 11. When analyzing data from experiments that involve more than two groups _________.

a. doing t tests on all possible pairs of means decreases the probability of making Type I errors
b. doing t tests on all possible pairs of means increases the probability of making Type I errors
c. it is generally permissible to do t tests between all possible pairs of means and use Student's t distribution
d. doing t tests on all possible pairs of means increases the probability of making Type II errors

e 12. The alternative hypothesis for which F_{obt} is appropriate in the one-way ANOVA is _________.

a. always nondirectional
b. never nondirectional
c. sometimes directional
d. evaluated with a one-tailed probability value
e. a and b
f. b and d

b 13. The alternative hypothesis evaluated by F_{obt} in the one-way ANOVA states that _________.

a. all conditions have the same effect
b. one or more of the conditions have different effects
c. $\mu_1 = \mu_2 = u_3 = \mu_k$
d. $\mu_1 \neq \mu_2 \neq \mu_3 \neq \mu_k$
e. b and d

d 14. Which of the following is(are) true?

a. df for $s_W^2 = N - k$
b. df for $s_B^2 = k - 1$
c. $df_T = N - 1$
d. all of the above

a 15. The one-way ANOVA partitions the total variability into _________.

a. SS_W and SS_B
b. s_W^2 and s_B^2
c. SS_W and SS_T
d. SS_B and s_B^2

e 16. Which of the following would cause F_{obt} to increase?

a. an increase in the difference between the means
b. an increase in the within-groups variability
c. an increase in the magnitude of the independent variable's effect
d. a and b
e. a and c

c 17. If $df_B = 2$ and $df_W = 14$, using $\alpha = 0.05$, F_{crit} = _________.

a. 19.42
b. 4.60
c. 3.74
d. 6.51

d 18. s_B^2 is a measure of _________.

a. σ^2 alone
b. σ^2 + the effects of the independent variable
c. the variability between the means
d. b and c

d 19. The two-way analysis of variance _________.

a. assesses the effects of two independent variables in one experiment
b. allows an assessment of the interaction between two independent variables
c. results in calculation of three *F* ratio's
d. all of the above
e. a and b

e 20. Which of the following are called "main effects" in a two-way analysis of variance?

a. the effect of Factor *A*
b. the effect of Factor *B*
c. the interaction of Factors *A* and *B*
d. all of the above
e. a and b

d 21. In a two-way ANOVA, if there is a significant interaction between Factor *A* and Factor *B*, which of the following may be true?

a. the effect of Factor *A* is not the same at all levels of Factor *B*
b. The effect of Factor *B* is not the same at all levels of Factor *A*
c. the effects of the two Factors do not differ across levels
d. a and/or b
e. need more information

a 22. The row variance estimate s_R^2 and the column variance estimate s_C^2 are used to measure _________.

a. the main effects of the independent variables
b. the interaction effects of the independent variables
c. a and b
d. none of the above

Questions 23 - 29 pertain to the following data.

An investigator conducts an experiment involving the effects of three levels of a drug on memory. Subjects are randomly assigned to one of three conditions. A different drug level is administered in each condition. Memory is measured 10 minutes after each subject receives the drug. The following scores are recorded. The higher the score, the better the memory.

Drug Level		
1	**2**	**3**
6	**9**	**14**
10	**7**	**13**
8	**9**	**15**
12	**13**	**19**

c 23. SS_B = ________.

a. 94.2
b. 96.0
c. 96.5
d. 97.4

b 24. SS_W = ________.

a. 62.25
b. 59.75
c. 56.65
d. 57.00

a 25. s_B^2 = ________.

a. 48.250
b. 50.145
c. 51.254
d. 45.750

d 26. s_W^2= ________.

a. 6.813
b. 6.558
c. 6.702
d. 6.639

c 27. F_{obt} = _________.

a. 8.31
b. 7.30
c. 7.27
d. 6.45

b 28. Using $\alpha = 0.05$, F_{crit} = _________.

a. 8.02
b. 4.26
c. 19.38
d. 4.46

b 29. Using $\alpha = 0.05$, what do you conclude?

a. reject H_0; the drug has the same effect on memory at all levels
b. reject H_0; the drug does not have the same effect on memory at all levels
c. retain H_0; we cannot conclude that the drug affects memory
d. accept H_0; the drug has no effect on memory

a 30. Estimate the size of the effect. $\hat{\omega}^2$ = ________.

a. 0.5109
b. 0.5210
c. 0.5100
d. 0.4328

Short Answer Questions

1. The analysis of variance is a nondirectional technique and yet it uses a one-tailed evaluation. Is this statement correct? If so, how can you explain this apparent contradiction?

2. The analysis of variance technique analyzes the variability of the data. Yet a significant *F* value indicates there is at least one significant mean difference between the conditions. How does analyzing the variability of the data allow conclusions about the means of the conditions?

3. In the two-way ANOVA, what is a main effect? What is an interaction?

4. Describe the sampling distribution of *F*.

True-False Questions

T 1. Tabled *F* values are one-tailed probability levels.

T 2. The *F* distribution has no negative values.

T 3. Variance ratio is the statistic underlying the *F* distribution.

T 4. The *F* distribution is a family of curves, each uniquely determined by df.

F 5. The *F* test is not used when comparing 2 or more estimates of the H_0 population variance.

T 6. The total variability of a set of data can be completely partitioned into the between-groups variability and the within-groups variability.

F 7. The within-groups variability increases necessarily as the between-groups variability increases.

F 8. The total variance of a set of data can be completely partitioned into the between-groups variance and the within-groups variance.

T 9. In the analysis of variance, the larger F_{obt} is (df constant), the lower the probability that the results of the experiment are due to chance.

T 10. When there are only two groups, then $t_{obt}^2 = F_{obt}$

T 11. The null hypothesis in the analysis of variance states that $\mu_1 = \mu_2 = \mu_3 = u_k$

F 12. The sampling distribution of *F* is a family of positively skewed curves each with a mean equal to 0.

T 13. $F_{obt} = s_B^2/s_W^2$

F 14. If $F_{obt} < F_{crit}$, we reject H_0.

F 15. In the one-way ANOVA, it is assumed that the within-groups variance estimate (s_W^2) is sensitive to the effect of the independent variable.

T 16. $SS_T = SS_W + SS_B$

T 17. The one-way ANOVA assumes $\sigma_1 2 = \sigma_2 2 = \sigma_3 2 = \sigma_k 2$

T 18. If $F < 1$, the independent variable has not had a significant effect.

F 19. The partition of variability is based on the idea that the deviation of each score from the Grand mean is made up of two parts; the deviation of each score from its group mean and the deviation of the other scores in the group from the group mean.

F 20. A significant F_{obt} value indicates that all the group means are significantly different from each other.

T 21. A factorial experiment is one in which the effect of two or more factors is assessed in one experiment.

F 22. In a two-way ANOVA, there are three possible main effects and one interaction.

T 23. In a two-way ANOVA, it is possible to have significant main effects without a significant interaction.

T 24. If there is an interaction between the variables of activity level and time of day, this means that activity level does not have the same effect at different times of day.

CHAPTER 16

MULTIPLE COMPARISONS

Multiple Choice Questions

d 1. *A priori* comparisons _________.

a. are planned in advance of the experiment
b. often arise out of theory and prior research
c. may be done without obtaining a significant F_{obt} in the one-way ANOVA
d. all of the above

d 2. In doing planned comparisons, we use _________.

a. the *t* test for independent groups, unaltered
b. the *t* test for independent groups with s_W^2 in the denominator
c. df equal to those of s_W^2
d. b and c

a 3. When doing planned comparisons, _________.

a. there is no correction for the inflated Type I error probability
b. a different number of df are used which corrects for the inflated Type I error probability
c. t_{obt} is reduced to correct for the inflated Type I error probability
d. a different sampling distribution is used to correct for the inflated Type I error probability

b 4. *A posteriori* or *post hoc* comparisons _________.

a. are planned before the experiment
b. are often decided on after the data are collected
c. require a significant F_{obt} before they may be conducted
d. b and c
e. all of the above

e 5. Which of the following is(are) statistical test(s) for doing *post hoc* comparisons?

a. HSD test
b. Newman-Keuls test
c. independent *t* test
d. two group one-way ANOVA
e. a and b
f. all of the above

b 6. The HSD test _________.

a. maintains the comparison-wise error rate at alpha
b. maintains the experiment-wise Type I error rate at alpha
c. is used for *a priori* comparisons
d. all of the above
e. b and c

c 7. Using the HSD test, if there are 16 df associated with s_W^2, and $\alpha = .05$ and the number of groups = 3, Q_{crit} = _________.

a. 4.13
b. 3.00
c. 3.65
d. 4.79

a 8. Using the Newman-Keuls test, if the number of means encompassed is 3, $\alpha = .05$, and there are 20 df associated with s_W^2, Q_{crit} = _________.

a. 3.58
b. 2.95
c. 4.02
d. 4.64

c 9. Within a single experiment, the value of Q_{crit} changes from comparison-to-comparison in the _________.

a. *t* test for independent groups
b. HSD test
c. Newman-Keuls test
d. all of the above

b 10. Orthogonal comparisons are a type of _________.

a. *a posteriori* comparisons
b. planned comparisons
c. regression analysis
d. none of the above

For questions 11 - 21, use the information relevant to questions 23 - 29 in Chapter 15 of this manual.

b 11. Assume you wanted to compare drug levels 2 and 3 using planned comparisons and a nondirectional H_1. The obtained value of the appropriate statistic is _________.

a. $Q_{obt} = 4.46$
b. $t_{obt} = -3.16$
c. $t_{obt} = -3.15$
d. $t_{obt} = -0.55$

c 12. The appropriate df = _________.

a. 11
b. 6
c. 9
d. 7

a 13. Using $\alpha = .05$, the critical value is _________.

a. ±2.262
b. −1.833
c. ±2.228
d. 3.95
e. 3.20

d 14. Using $\alpha = .05$, what is your conclusion?

a. accept H_0; the drug has the same effect at these levels
b. retain H_0; we cannot conclude the drug has a different effect at these levels
c. reject H_0; the groups are not significantly different
d. reject H_0; the drug has different effects at these levels

b 15. Assume you are going to do a *post hoc* comparison between drug levels 2 and 3 using the HSD test. The obtained value of the appropriate statistic is _________.

a. $t_{obt} = -3.16$
b. $Q_{obt} = 4.46$
c. $Q_{obt} = -4.46$
d. $Q_{obt} = 5.25$

c 16. Using $\alpha = .05$, the appropriate critical value is _________.

a. ±2.179
b. 3.20
c. 3.95
d. 5.43

b 17. Using $\alpha = .05$, what is your conclusion?

a. retain H_0; we cannot conclude the drug has a different effect at these levels
b. reject H_0; the drug has different effects at these levels
c. retain H_0; the drug has the same effect at these levels
d. reject H_0; the groups are not significantly different

b 18. Assume you are going to do a *post hoc* comparison between drug levels 2 and 3 using the Newman-Keuls test. The obtained value of the appropriate statistic is ________.

a. $t_{obt} = -3.16$
b. $Q_{obt} = 4.46$
c. $Q_{obt} = 3.30$
d. $Q_{obt} = 5.25$

c 19. The df = ________.

a. 8
b. 6
c. 9
d. 11

b 20. Using $\alpha = .05$, the critical value is ________.

a. ±2.179
b. 3.20
c. 3.95
d. 4.60

b 21. Using $\alpha = .05$, what do you conclude?

a. retain H_0; we cannot conclude the drug has a different effect at these levels
b. reject H_0; the drug has different effects at these levels
c. retain H_0; the drug has the same effect at these levels
d. reject H_0; the groups are not significantly different

True-False Questions

T 1. Planned comparisons are the same thing as *a priori* comparisons.

F 2. When doing planned comparisons, the denominator of the t equation changes for each pair of means compared.

T 3. *A posteriori* or *post hoc* comparisons are the same thing.

T 4. With *a priori* comparisons, there is no correction for the inflated probability of making a Type I error.

T 5. Both the HSD and the Newman-Keuls test use the Studentized Range distributions.

F 6. The experiment-wise error rate is the probability of making a Type I error for any of the possible comparisons.

F 7. The HSD test uses the t_{obt} statistic.

T 8. It is possible to get significant differences between pairs of means using the Newman-Keuls test that are not significant using the HSD test.

T 9. When using multiple comparisons, *a priori* comparisons are more powerful than either the HSD or the Newman-Keuls tests.

F 10. In using the HSD test, it is necessary to rank order the means.

T 11. When using multiple comparisons, the real issue is between doing the most powerful test and making the fewest Type I errors.

F 12. Q_{crit} is generally the same for the HSD and the Newman-Keuls tests.

F 13. The HSD and Newman-Keuls tests differ in the value they calculate for Q_{obt}.

T 14. The appropriate sampling distribution for the HSD test is the Studentized Range distribution.

F 15. When comparisons are planned in advance of conducting the experiment, you need a significant value for F_{obt} before you can make the comparisons.

F 16. When doing *post hoc* comparisons, it is necessary to have a significant value for F_{obt} before you can make the comparisons.

CHAPTER 17

INTRODUCTION TO THE TWO-WAY ANALYSIS OF VARIANCE

Multiple Choice Questions

c 1. A significant interaction effect occurs when _________.

a. there are no main effects
b. variable *A* has a main effect and variable *B* does not
c. the combined effects of variables *A* and *B* yield an unexpected effect
d. none of the above

f 2. The null hypothesis for the two-way ANOVA asserts that _________.

a. the within-cells variance estimate is an estimate of σ^2
b. $\mu_{a_1} = \mu_{a_2} = \mu_{a_3} = \mu_{a_r}$
c. $\mu_{b_1} = \mu_{b_2} = \mu_{b_3} = \mu_{b_c}$
d. $\mu_{a_1 b_1} = \mu_{a_1 b_2} = \mu_{a_r b_c}$
e. all of the above
f. b, c and d

a 3. Which of the following increase(s) as the effect of the *A* variable increases?

a. s_R^2
b. s_C^2
c. s_W^2
d. s_{RC}^2

b 4. Which of the following increase(s) as the effect of the *B* variable increases?

a. s_R^2
b. s_C^2
c. s_W^2
d. s_{RC}^2

d 5. Which of the following increase(s) as the interaction effect increases?

a. s_R^2
b. s_C^2
c. s_W^2
d. s_{RC}^2

e 6. If the null hypothesis is correct, which of the following is (are) an estimate of σ^2?

a. s_R^2
b. s_C^2
c. s_W^2
d. s_{RC}^2
e. all of the above

c 7. If there are no main effects, then _________.

a. s_C^2/s_W^2 is less than F_{crit}
b. s_R^2/s_W^2 is less than F_{crit}
c. s_{RC}^2/s_W^2 is less than F_{crit}
d. a and b
e. b and c

d 8. If the *A* variable has a real effect, _________.

a. s_C^2/s_W^2 must equal or exceed F_{crit}
b. s_R^2/s_W^2 must equal or exceed F_{crit}
c. it is possible that s_C^2/s_W^2 is less than F_{crit}
d. it is possible that s_R^2/s_W^2 is less than F_{crit}

b 9. A main effect for variable *A* means that _________.

a. the effect of variable *A* is the same over all levels of variable *B*
b. the effect of variable *A* is significant when averaged over all levels of variable *B*
c. the effect of variable A is not the same over all levels of variable *B*
d. variable *A* has a greater effect than variable *B*

d 10. The two-way analysis of variance _________.

a. assesses the effects of two independent variables in one experiment
b. allows an assessment of the interaction between two independent variables
c. results in calculation of three *F* ratio's
d. all of the above
e. a and b

e 11. Which of the following are called "main effects" in a two-way analysis of variance?

a. the effect of Factor *A*
b. the effect of Factor *B*
c. the interaction of Factors *A* and *B*
d. all of the above
e. a and b

d 12. In a two-way ANOVA, if there is a significant interaction between Factor *A* and Factor *B*, which of the following may be true?

a. the effect of Factor *A* is not the same at all levels of Factor *B*
b. The effect of Factor *B* is not the same at all levels of Factor *A*
c. the effects of the two Factors do not differ across levels
d. a and/or b
e. need more information

a 13. The row variance estimate s_R^2 and the column variance estimate s_C^2 are used to measure _________.

a. the main effects of the independent variables
b. the interaction effects of the independent variables
c. a and b
d. none of the above

For questions 14 - 22, refer to the following material.

An investigator collects the following data on variables *A* and *B*, using a two-way independent groups design. Use α = .05 in analyzing the data.

Variable *A*	Variable *B* (1)	(2)	(3)
	10	13	15
	12	15	19
(1)	14	17	20
	18	22	25
	17	16	19
	15	18	26
	17	19	30
(2)	19	22	31
	23	27	36
	20	21	29

c 14. F_{obt} for the *A* variable equals ________.

a. 2.66
b. 16.34
c. 29.11
d. 11.23

b 15. F_{obt} for the *B* variable equals ________.

a. 2.66
b. 16.34
c. 29.11
d. 11.23

a 16. F_{obt} for the interaction equals ________.

a. 2.66
b. 16.34
c. 29.11
d. 11.23

d 17. F_{crit} for the *A* variable equals ________.

a. 3.40
b. 7.82
c. 5.81
d. 4.26

a 18. F_{crit} for the B variable equals ________.

a. 3.40
b. 7.82
c. 5.81
d. 4.26

a 19. F_{crit} for the interaction equals _________.

a. 3.40
b. 7.82
c. 5.81
d. 4.26

b 20. The conclusion regarding the *A* variable is _________.

a. retain H_0; chance is a reasonable explanation
b. reject H_0; there is a significant main effect for variable *A*
c. accept H_0; variable *A* has no real effect
d. reject H_0; chance is a reasonable explanation

c 21. The conclusion regarding the *B* variable is _________.

a. reject H_0; variable *B* has no effect
b. retain H_0; chance is a reasonable explanation
c. reject H_0; there is a significant main effect for variable *B*
d. accept H_0; chance is a reasonable explanation

a 22. The conclusion regarding the interaction is _________.

a. retain H_0; chance is a reasonable explanation
b. accept H_0; chance is a reasonable explanation
c. reject H_0; there is a significant interaction between variables *A* and *B*
d. reject H_0; there is no interaction between variables *A* and *B*

True-False Questions

T 1. In two-way ANOVA, SS_T is partitioned into SS_R, SS_W, SS_C and SS_{RC}.

F 2. The within-cells variance estimate measures treatment effects.

F 3. The row variance estimate does not change as the effect of the independent variable increases.

T 4. The column variance estimate increases as the effect of the independent variable increases.

T 5. A significant interaction effect occurs when the effects of one of the variables is not the same at all levels of the other variable.

T 6. Differences among cell means are used to assess the interaction effect.

F 7. Differences among row means are used to assess the interaction effect.

T 8. Differences among column means are used to assess the main effect of one of the variables

T 9. SS_W for one-way ANOVA and SS_W for two-way ANOVA are conceptually similar.

T 10. SS_B for one-way ANOVA is conceptually similar to SS_R and SS_C for two-way ANOVA.

F 11. $SS_T = SS_R + SS_C + SS_W$

F 12. It is not possible to have a significant interaction effect unless one of the variables also has a significant main effect.

T 13. A "mean square" is the same thing as a "variance estimate".

F 14. The homogeneity of variance assumption assumes the population scores from which each of the samples are drawn are normally distributed.

F 15. A two factor experiment yields no more information than two single factor experiments.

CHAPTER 18

CHI-SQUARE AND OTHER NONPARAMETRIC TESTS

Multiple Choice Questions

a 1. Chi-square is used to test differences between _________.

a. proportions
b. means
c. variances
d. none of the above

f 2. The larger the discrepancy between f_o and f_e for each cell, _________.

a. the more likely the results will not be significant
b. the more likely H_0 will be rejected
c. the more likely the population proportions are the same
d. the more likely the population proportions are different
e. a and c
f. b and d

c 3. For any given alpha level, χ^2_{crit} _________.

a. increases with increases in N
b. decreases with increases in N
c. increases with increases in degrees of freedom
d. a and c

b 4. Chi-square should not be used if _________.

a. df = 1
b. f_e is below 5
c. f_o is below 5
d. $f_e = f_o$

e 5. Chi-square may be used with _________

a. nominal data
b. ordinal data
d. interval data
d. ratio data
e. all of the above

a 6. To compute χ^2, the entries in the contingency table should be _________.

a. frequencies
b. means
c. variances
d. degrees of freedom

b 7. The degrees of freedom for a contingency table equal _________.

a. $rc - 1$
b. $(r - 1)(c - 1)$
c. $(r - 1)(c)$
d. $(c - 1)(r)$
e. $N - 1$

c 8. In most situations, parametric tests _________.

a. have the same power as nonparametric tests
b. are less powerful than nonparametric tests
c. are more powerful than nonparametric tests
d. are less sensitive than nonparametric tests
e. b and d

f 9. Which of the following are examples of parametric tests?

a. *t* test
b. sign test
c. Mann-Whitney *U* test
d. Chi-square test
e. *F* test
f. a and e

f 10. Which of the following are examples of nonparametric tests?

a. *t* test
b. sign test
c. Mann-Whitney *U* test
d. Chi-square test
e. *F* test
f. b, c and d
g. all of the above

d 11. Which of the following are true?

a. f_o is the symbol for the observed frequency
b. f_e is the symbol for the expected frequency
c. χ^2 is the symbol for chi-square
d. all of the above

d 12. The sampling distribution of chi-square is _________.

a. skewed
b. varies with df
c. is a theoretical distribution
d. all of the above
e. a and b

c 13. The χ^2 test is _________.

a. always directional
b. never directional
c. generally nondirectional
d. generally directional

b 14. When evaluating χ^2_{obt}, the critical region for rejection of H_0 _________.

a. lies under both tails of the distribution
b. lies under the right hand tail of the distribution
c. lies under the left hand tail of the distribution
d. lies in the middle of the distribution

e 15. A contingency table _________.

a. is a two-way table
b. involves two variables
c. involves two mutually exclusive variables
d. all of the above
e. a and b

a 16. The computation of f_e _________.

a. is based on population proportion estimates
b. is based on known population proportions
c. is based on population means
d. none of the above

c 17. In a 2 x 2 contingency table, if we keep the marginals at their observed values, how many f_o scores are free to vary?

a. 3
b. 0
c. 1
d. all of them

e 18. The Wilcoxin signed ranks test _________.

a. is used with a correlated groups design
b. is used with data that is nominal in scaling
c. uses both the magnitude and direction of the data
d. all of the above
e. a and b

a 19. If $N = 18$ and $\alpha = 0.05_{2\ \text{tailed}}$, the value of T_{crit} is _________.

a. 40
b. ±40
c. −40
d. 47

a 20. If $\alpha = 0.05$, and df = 4, the value of χ^2_{crit} = _________.

a. 9.488
b. 0.711
c. 7.815
d. 11.070

For questions 21 - 24 refer to the following information.

Prior to a recent gubernatorial election, a survey was conducted to determine whether there was a relationship between sexual gender and preference for the Democratic or Republican candidate. The following data were recorded.

	Candidate Preference		
	Republican	**Democrat**	
Female	**82**	**118**	**200**
Male	**68**	**132**	**200**
	150	**250**	**400**

c 21. The value of χ^2_{obt} = _________.

a. 2.06
b. 2.09
c. 1.80
d. 1.75

b 22. The value of df = __________.

a. 2
b. 1
c. 3
d. need more information

a 23. Using $\alpha = 0.05$, χ^2_{crit} = __________.

a. 3.841
b. 5.412
c. 2.706
d. –3.841

c 24. Using $\alpha = 0.05$, what is your conclusion?

a. accept H_0; there is no relationship between sex and candidate preference
b. reject H_0; there is a significant relationship between sex and candidate preference
c. retain H_0; the study does not show a significant relationship between sex and candidate preference
d. retain H_0; this study shows a significant relationship between sex and candidate preference

For questions 25 - 27 refer to the following information

A study is conducted to determine whether sunshine affects depression. Eight individuals are given a questionnaire measuring depression immediately following a run of 10 consecutive days when the sun shone for over 80% of the daylight hours. The same individuals have their depression measured immediately following 10 consecutive days without any sunshine. The following data are collected. The higher the score the greater the depression.

Individuals	1	2	3	4	5	6	7	8
Sunshine	10	12	14	11	12	10	14	15
No sunshine	20	21	17	14	18	8	18	14

b 25. Using the Wilcoxin signed ranks test, the value of T_{obt} is __________.

a. −3
b. 3
c. 33
d. 4

d 26. Using $\alpha = 0.05_{2\text{ tail}}$, T_{crit} = _________.

a. 2
b. 5
c. ±3
d. 3

a 27. Using $\alpha = 0.05_{2\text{ tail}}$, what do you conclude? Assume for the purpose of this question, that sunshine was the only systematic difference between the conditions.

a. reject H_0; sunshine appears to affect depression
b. reject H_0 ; sunshine has no effect on depression
c. retain H_0; we cannot conclude that sunshine affects depression
d. accept H_0; sunshine affects depression

e 28. Which of the following are nonparametric tests?

a. sign test
b. Wilcoxin test
c. Mann-Whitney *U* test
d. Kruskal-Wallis test
e. all of the above
f. a, b and c

f 29. The Mann-Whitney *U* test can be used with _________.

a. nominal data
b. interval data
c. ordinal data
d. ratio data
e. all of the above
f. b, c and d

a 30. Generally, if R_1 is greater than R_2, _________.

a. the equation $U = n_1 n_2 + \frac{n_1(n_1+1)}{2} - R_1$ yields the *U* value
b. the equation $U = n_1 n_2 + \frac{n_2(n_2+1)}{2} - R_2$ yields the *U* value
c. the power of the test is necessarily low
d. we must reject H_0

b 31. As the separation between the two groups of scores increases, U_{obt} _________.

a. increases
b. decreases
c. stays the same
d. approaches U'_{obt}

c 32. In the Mann-Whitney *U* test, the *U* value of 0 _________.

a. represents a low degree of separation between the two groups
b. implies that the two groups are identical
c. represents the greatest degree of separation between the two groups
d. indicates that the power of the experiment is very low.

d 33. The statistics (*U* or *U'*) used in the Mann-Whitney *U* test, measure _________.

a. the differences between the means of the two groups
b. the direction of the differences between pairs of scores
c. the power of the experiment
d. the separation between the two groups

d 34. A Mann-Whitney *U* value of zero indicates _________.

a. you can reject the null hypothesis
b. low degree of separation between the scores of each group
c. zero difference between the two groups
d. high degree of separation between the scores of each group

c 35. $U + U'$ equals _________.

a. n
b. $n_1 + n_2$
c. $n_1 \times n_2$
d. none of the above

a 36. The Mann-Whitney *U* test is used with _________.

a. an independent groups design
b. a replicated measures design
c. a correlated groups design
d. b and c

c 37. The Mann-Whitney *U* test uses _________.

a. only the direction of the scores
b. only the magnitude of the scores
c. both the magnitude and direction of the scores
d. none of the above

d 38. Consider the following set of scores: 25, 28, 28, 28, 30. In assigning ranks to the scores, a score of 28 receives a rank of _________.

a. 2.5
b. 2
c. 4
d. 3

b 39. Using the data in question 11, a score of 30 would receive a rank of _________.

a. 4
b. 5
c. 3
d. 0

b 40. If $n_1 = 5$, $n_2 = 4$, and $\alpha = 0.01_{2\text{ tail}}$, the power of the Mann-Whitney *U* test equals _________.

a. 1
b. 0
c. 0.01
d. need more information

a 41. If $n_1 = 6$, $n_2 = 8$ and $\alpha = 0.05_{2\text{ tail}}$, U_{crit} value is _________.

a. 8
b. 40
c. 6
d. 42

a 42. A student at a Midwest college is interested in whether Psychology majors spend more or less time studying than English majors. She randomly selects 8 Psychology majors and 8 English majors and determines their weekly studying time. The following are the scores. Note one person dropped out of the study.

Psychology Majors	**16**	**12**	**13**	**10**	**9**	**10**	**8**	
English Majors	**10**	**25**	**15**	**17**	**23**	**14**	**19**	**18**

The value of U_{obt} is _________.

a. 6
b. 50
c. 14
d. 42

b 43. In question 42, if $\alpha = 0.05_{2\text{ tail}}$, U_{crit} = _________.

a. 7
b. 10
c. 46
d. 49

a 44. Using $\alpha = 0.05_{2\text{ tail}}$, what do you conclude regarding the data given in question 42?

a. reject H_0; there is a significant difference in the amount of time Psychology and English majors study
b. reject H_0; there is no difference in the amount of time Psychology and English majors study
c. accept H_0; there is no difference in the amount of time Psychology and English majors study
d. retain H_0; there is no difference in the amount of time Psychology and English majors study

b 45. The statistic used with the Kruskal-Wallis test is _________.

a. F_{obt}
b. H_{obt}
c. U_{obt}
d. t_{obt}

For questions 46-48, refer to the following material.

A researcher conducts a one-way ANOVA involving three groups. When she analyzes the data she realizes the data seriously violate the assumptions underlying parametric ANOVA. Therefor, she decides to use the Kruskal-Wallis test to conclude with regard to H_0. The data are given below.

(1)	(2)	(3)
6	8	12
10	12	13
12	9	20
16	15	18
14	17	22
7	11	15

b 46. H_{obt} = _________.

a. 4.25
b. 5.43
c. 2.68
d. 6.86

c 47. Using $\alpha = 0.05$, H_{crit} = ________.

a. 9.210
b. 7.815
c. 5.991
d. 7.824

d 48. What is the appropriate conclusion concerning H_0?

a. reject H_0; the independent variable has a real effect
b. accept H_0; the independent variable has no effect
c. retain H_0; the independent variable has a real effect
d. retain H_0; we cannot conclude the independent variable has a real effect

Short Answer Questions

1. What distinguishes parametric from nonparametric tests? Give some examples.

2 When might we use a nonparametric test? Give an example?

3. What are the assumptions underlying the Kruskal-Wallis test?

4 What are the assumptions underlying the chi-square test?

5. What are the assumptions underlying the Mann-Whitney U test?

6 What are the assumptions underlying the Wilcoxin signed ranks test?

True-False Questions

T 1. All inference tests depend on population characteristics.

F 2. Parametric tests depend less on population characteristics than nonparametric tests.

T 3. Parametric tests are more versatile than nonparametric tests.

T 4. χ^2_{obt} cannot be negative.

T 5. To find f_e for any cell, multiply the marginals for that cell and divide by N.

F 6. The Wilcoxin signed ranks test is less powerful than the sign test.

T 7. To use the Wilcoxin signed ranks test, the difference scores must be at least of ordinal scaling.

T 8. An assumption of χ^2 is that the scores in each cell are independent.

F 9. The Wilcoxin signed ranks test is more powerful than the *t* test for correlated groups.

F 10. Using χ^2, the closer the observed frequency of each cell is to the expected frequency for that cell, the higher the probability of rejecting H_0.

T 11. In order to reject the null hypothesis, $\chi^2_{obt} \geq \chi^2_{crit}$.

T 12. The χ^2 distribution is a family of curves that vary with degrees of freedom.

T 13. The χ^2 test answers questions about population proportions.

T 14. For valid use of chi-square, each subject can only have one entry in the table, and the table entries must be frequencies.

F 15. Parametric tests are always more desirable than nonparametric tests.

T 16. The Mann-Whitney *U* test makes no assumption about the shape of the population scores.

F 17. The Mann-Whitney *U* test is used with a repeated measures design.

F 18. If U_{obt} and U'_{obt} are equal, there is little overlap between the groups.

T 19. $U = 0$ is the lowest possible *U* value.

T 20. $U = 0$ indicates the greatest degree of separation between the groups.

F 21 Generally, $U'_{obt} < U_{obt}$

F 22. The Mann-Whitney *U* test can only be used to analyze directional alternative hypotheses.

T 23. The Mann-Whitney *U* test analyzes the separation between the groups.

F 24. The data must be at least interval in scaling to use the Mann-Whitney *U* test.

T 25. The Mann-Whitney *U* test uses both the magnitude and direction of the scores.

T 26. U_{obt} and U'_{obt} yield the same information with regard to the degree of separation.

T 27. The Kruskal-Wallis test is used as a substitute for parametric one-way ANOVA.

F 28. The Kruskal-Wallis test assumes population normality.

T 29. The Kruskal-Wallis test requires only ordinal scaling of the dependent variable.

F 30. When using the Kruskal-Wallis test, tied scores between conditions are thrown out.

T 31. The Kruskal-Wallis test requires there are at least 5 scores in each sample.

Answers to Selected Textbook Problems

The answers to most end-of-chapter problems are given in the text in Appendix C. However, I have withheld answers to at least one problem in each chapter, due to requests from many professors. The answers to these problems are given below.

Chapter 1

6. a. (1) fear of smoking (2) number of cigarettes smoked (3) the 40 smoking adults who participated in the experiment (4) all smoking adults residing in the city where the psychologist works at the time of the experiment (5) the number of cigarettes smoked daily by each member of the sample during the 2-month post-film period (6) the mean number of cigarettes smoked daily by each group.

9. b. The sample scores are the 15 weights given. The population scores are the 450 weights that would result if all the hamburgers served on that day were measured.

Chapter 2

5. c. 148
6. b. 25.26
7. c. 95-105
8. c. 58
13. c. 52

Chapter 3

8. b. 19.74
12. b. 17.16

15a.

Class Interval	f
3.6-3.8	3
3.3-3.5	12
3.0-3.2	14
2.7-2.9	10
2.4-2.6	7
2.1-2.3	6
1.8-2.0	5
1.5-1.7	3
1.2-1.4	3
0.9-1.1	1
	64

Chapter 4

16. b. $\overline{X}$ = 22.75, Mdn = 24.5, mode = 30
27. b. range = 24, s = 10.76, s^2 = 115.70
28. 92.20

Chapter 5

14. a. 89.44% **b.** 8.38% **c.** 80.18% **d.** 26.84% **e.** 123.12

Chapter 6

15. b. r = 0.63 **c.** Not very well. It only accounts for 39.63% of the variability of the Exam 1 scores.

Chapter 7

9. b. $Y' = 0.316X - 0.015$ **c.** $X' = 1.105Y + 6.526$ **e.** 3.77

Chapter 8

14. a. 0.0278 **b.** 0.0556 **c.** 0.5556 **d.** 0.1667
24. a. 0.0084 **b.** 0.1334 **c.** 0.7422

Chapter 9

9. a. 0.2312 **b.** 0.3186 **c.** 0.2184
12. 0.0006

Chapter 10

9. a. The alternative hypothesis states that rhesus monkeys have a preference for either novel stimulation or repetitive stimulation. **b.** The null hypothesis states that in rhesus monkeys there is no difference in preference between novel and repetitive stimulation. **c.** p(0, 1, 2, 10, 11, or 12 pluses) = 0.0384. Since 0.0384 < 0.05, you can reject H_0. Rhesus monkeys appear to prefer novel stimulation. **d.** You may be making a Type I error, rejecting H_0 if it is true. **e.** The results apply to the rhesus monkeys housed in the university colony at the time of the experiment.

Chapter 11

7. Power = 0.2969, beta = 0.7031

Chapter 12

21. a. The alternative hypothesis states that the student's technique affects the duration that schizophrenics spend in an institution. **b.** The null hypothesis states the student's technique has no effect on the duration that schizophrenics spend in an institution. **c.** $z_{obt} = -2.09$, and $z_{crit} = \pm 1.96$. Since $|z_{obt}| > 1.96$, you reject H_0 and accept H_1. The student's technique appears to shorten the duration of stay.

Chapter 13

14. b. 117.01-122.99 (95%) ; 115.97-124.03 (99%)

16. a. The alternative hypothesis states that the effectiveness of training in mathematics at the private high school differs from that of the public high schools. **b.** The null hypothesis states that the private high school and the public high schools are equal in the effectiveness of the mathematics training they provide. **c.** $t_{obt} = 2.62$, and $t_{crit} = \pm 2.021$. Since $|t_{obt}| > 2.021$, you reject H_0 and conclude that the effectiveness of training in mathematics at the private high school does differ from that of the public high schools. It appears to be better.

Chapter 14

14. a. The alternative hypothesis states that the experimental birth control pill affects blood pressure, $\mu_D \neq 0$. **b.** The null hypothesis states that the birth control pill has no effect on blood pressure, $\mu_D = 0$. **c.** $t_{obt} = 1.52$, and $t_{crit} = \pm 3.250$. Since $|t_{obt}| < 3.250$, you retain H_0. The data are insufficient to allow you to conclude that the birth control pill affects blood pressure.

16. a. $t_{obt} = 4.00$, and $t_{crit} = 2.602$. You reject H_0 and conclude that the level of lead in the blood of children living near the smelter is significantly higher than that of children living in an area relatively free from possible lead pollution. b. $\hat{\omega}^2 = 0.469$, accounting for 46.9% of the variability. No, the effect is a moderate one.

Chapter 15

17. a.

Source	SS	df	s^2	F_{obt}
Between	1962.133	2	981.066	14.06
Within	837.200	12	69.767	
Total	2799.333	14		

F_{crit} = 3.88. Since F_{obt} >3.88, we reject H_0 and conclude that sleep deprivation has an effect on the ability to maintain sustained attention.

d. $\hat{\omega}^2 = 0.635$, accounting for 63.5% of the variability.

Chapter 16

7. **a.** t_{obt} = 5.30, and t_{crit} = ±2.179. Reject H_0 and conclude that 48 hours of sleep deprivation significantly affects the ability to maintain sustained concentration. It appears to decrease this ability. **b.**

	Sleep Deprivation		
Condition	48 hr	24 hr	Normal Sleep
$\overline{X}$	48.6	61.8	76.6
$\overline{X}_i - \overline{X}_j$		14.8	28.0 13.2
Q_{obt}		3.96	7.50 3.53
Q_{crit}		3.08	3.77 3.08

Reject H_0 for all three comparisons. Forty-eighty hours of sleep deprivation produces the greatest decrement in the ability to maintain sustained attention. The effect is also seen at 24 hours of deprivation, although it is not as strong.

c.

	Sleep Deprivation		
Condition	48 hr	24 hr	Normal Sleep
$\overline{X}$	48.6	61.8	76.6
$\overline{X}_i - \overline{X}_j$		14.8	28.0 13.2
Q_{obt}		3.96	7.50 3.53
Q_{crit} = 3.77			

Reject H_0 for normal sleep compared with 24-hour and 48-hour sleep deprivation. Retain H_0 with regard to the 24-hour and 48-hour sleep deprivation comparison. Twenty-four- and 48-hour sleep deprivation significantly interferes with the ability to maintain sustained attention. Since the mean of the 48-hour sleep-deprived group is considerably lower than the mean of the 24-hour sleep-deprived group, failure to find a significant difference between these two conditions is probably due to the relatively low power of the HSD test. Note that this comparison was significant using the Newman-Keuls test. Since the Newman-Keuls test adjusts Q_{crit} for each comparison, it is a more powerful test.

Chapter 17

9. **a.** There is no difference in the effect of the two fertilizers. $\mu_{a_1} = \mu_{a_2}$. There is no difference in the density of the three grasses. $\mu_{b_1} = \mu_{b_2} = \mu_{b_3}$. There is no interaction between the type of fertilizer and the type of grass. With any main effects removed, $\mu_{a_1b_1} = \mu_{a_1b_2} = \mu_{a_1b_3} = \mu_{a_2b_1} = \mu_{a_2b_2} = \mu_{a_2b_3}$. **b.**

Source	SS	df	s^2	F_{obt}	F_{crit}
Rows (type of fertilizer)	177.633	1	177.633	17.05	4.26
Columns (type of grass)	176.867	2	88.433	8.49	3.40
Rows × columns	2.467	2	1.233	0.12	3.40
Within-cells	250.000	24	10.417		
Total	606.967	29			

Since $F_{obt} > F_{crit}$ for both the row and column main effects, H_0 is rejected. There is a significant main effect for the type of fertilizer and the type of grass. The interaction was not significant ($F_{obt} < F_{crit}$). It is apparent from the pattern of cell means that type 1 fertilizer was superior to type 2 fertilizer. The pattern of cell means also shows that Green Velvet grass was superior to the other two types. Therefore, on the basis of this experiment, you recommend Green Velvet grass and type 1 fertilizer. (You also receive a bonus for such a nicely conducted experiment.)

Chapter 18

18. $\chi^2_{obt} = 18.00$, and $\chi^2_{crit} = 9.210$. Since $\chi^2_{obt} > 9.210$, we reject H_0. There is a relationship between these occupations and attitudes toward wage and price controls. Labor appears to be for the controls, business against the controls, and the professions fairly evenly divided.

29. **a.** The alternative hypothesis states that there is a difference in the degree of political conservatism of university theology and psychology professors. **b.** The null hypothesis states that university theology and psychology professors have the same degree of political conservatism. **c.** $U_{obt} = 19$, $U'_{obt} = 77$. Since $U_{obt} < 22$, you reject H_0 and conclude that theology and psychology professors differ in political conservatism. The theology professors appear to be more conservative.

Chapter 19

13. **a.** $z_{obt} = -1.11$. Since $z_{crit} = -1.645$, we must retain H_0. We cannot conclude that this year's freshmen have a lower daily fat intake level. **b.** Power = 0.5793 **c.** Power = 0.8315. **d.** $N = 38$ (rounded to nearest integer).

Computer Exercises

The material that follows is intended for use with a computer and assigned statistical software. The material is chapter specific.

Chapter 2

1. Use the assigned software to find the sum of each of the sets of scores shown below.
   a. 12, 15, 18, 14, 13, 18, 17, 23, 22, 14, 10.
   b. 1.3, 0.9, 2.2, 2.4, 3.2, 5.6, 7.8, 3.3, 2.6.
   c. 214, 113, 115, 314, 715, 423, 500, 125, 224, 873.
2. For the following data, use the assigned software to find $\sum_{i=1}^{N} X_i$
   a. 2.44, 3.57, 6.43, 3.21, 8.45, 6.37, 8.25, 3.98.
   b. 23, 65, 43, 87, 89, 64, 59, 67, 53, 34, 21, 18, 28.

Chapter 3

1. For this exercise, use the English exam scores of Problem 5 on p. 59 of the textbook.
   a. Use the assigned software to construct a histogram. Use the default number of intervals.
   b. Use the assigned software to construct a stem and leaf using the default interval width.
   c. Which looks better, the histogram or the stem and leaf diagram?
   d. Which gives more information?
2. Again use the English exam scores of Problem 4 of the textbook.
   a. This time employ the software to construct a histogram using 5 intervals instead of the number of intervals used by the default algorithm.
   b. Compare this histogram with the one you constructed in **1a**. Which do you prefer? Why?
3. Again, use the English exam scores of Problem 4.
   a. This time employ the software to construct a stem and leaf diagram using a interval width for each line of 10.
   b. Compare this stem and leaf diagram with the one you constructed in **1b**. Which do you prefer? Why?

4. Use the weight lost scores given in Problem 10 on p. 59 of the textbook.

    a. Use the software to construct a histogram using the default number of intervals.
    b. Next, use the software to construct a histogram using one half of the number of intervals as in **4a**.
    c. Next, use the software to construct a histogram using twice of the number of intervals as in part **4a**.
    d. Which gives the best picture? Why?
    e. Use the software to construct a stem and leaf diagram using the default interval width per line.
    f. Next, double the interval width per line and construct another stem and leaf diagram using the assigned software.
    g. Which stem and leaf diagram do you prefer? Why?

Chapter 4

1. Use the assigned software to compute the mean, standard deviation and variance for the following sets of scores:
    a. 8, 2, 6, 12, 4, 7, 4, 10, 13, 15, 11, 12, 5
    b. 7.2, 2.3, 5.4, 2.3, 3.4, 9.2, 7.6, 4.7, 2.8, 6.5
    c. 23, 65, 47, 38, 86, 57, 32, 66, 43, 85, 29, 40, 42
    d. 212, 334, 250, 436, 425, 531, 600, 487, 529, 234. 515

2. Does the software use *N or N* – 1 in the denominator when computing the standard deviation? How do you know?

3. Using the assigned software, demonstrate that the mean of a set of scores can vary without changing the standard deviation.

6. Using the assigned software, demonstrate that the standard deviation of a set of scores can vary without changing the mean.

Chapter 5

1. Use the assigned software to compute z scores for the following data sets:
    a. 10, 13, 15, 16, 18, 20, 21, 24
    b. 0.4, 1.2, 1.5, 1.8, 2.2, 2.4, 3.2, 3.6
    c. 0.22, 1.26, 1.31, 2.35, 3.38, 3.52, 4.02, 4.50, 5.24, 5.75

2. Use the assigned software to compute z scores for Problem 20, p. 97 in the textbook. Compare your answer with that given in Appendix C for this problem.

3. Beginning with a set of raw scores with *N* = 10, use the assigned software to demonstrate that the mean of the z transformed values equals 0 and the standard deviation equals 1.

Chapter 6

Chapter 6 of the textbook discusses the topic of correlation. Statistical software can be very helpful in this area by graphing scatter plots and computing correlation coefficients.

1. Use the assigned software to graph a scatter plot of the IQ and Grade Point Average (GPA) data given in the textbook in Table 6.2 on p. 105. For convenience the data have been reproduced here.

Student No.	1	2	3	4	5	6	7	8	9	10	11	12
GPA	1.0	1.6	1.2	2.1	2.6	1.8	2.6	2.0	3.2	2.6	3.0	3.6
IQ	110	112	118	119	122	125	127	130	132	134	136	138

   Compare your scatter plot with Figure 6.4 on p. 105

2. Use the assigned software to compute Pearson *r* for the IQ and GPA data. Compare the value obtained with the one presented in the textbook for Practice Problem 6.1 on p. 112.

3. Using the data given in Problem 18, p. 127 of the textbook:
   a. Use the assigned software to construct a scatter plot of the data given in Problem 18, p. 127 of the textbook. Use "American" as the X-axis variable, and "Italian" as the Y-axis variable.
   b. Describe the relationship.
   c. Use the assigned software to calculate the value of Pearson *r*.

4. Use assigned software to do Problem 16, p. 126 of the textbook. In constructing the scatter plot, use "Cigarettes Smoked" as the X-axis variable. It sure is a lot easier using the computer.

5. A psychology professor is interested in whether there is a relationship between reaction time (RT) and age. The following data are collected on thirty individuals randomly sampled from the city in which the professor works. Random sampling is conducted in a manner to assure that a wide age range is represented in the sample.
   a. Use the assigned software to construct a scatter plot of the data. Assign "RT" as the *Y* variable and "Age" as the *X* variable.
   b. Describe the relationship.
   c. Use the assigned software to compute Pearson *r*.
   d. How much of the variability of RT is accounted for by Age?

Subject No.	1	2	3	4	5	6	7	8	9	10
RT (msec)	300	538	832	747	610	318	822	693	461	460
Age (yrs)	24.6	28.5	45.2	31.1	22.0	14.4	57.9	55.0	37.3	14.0

Subject No.	11	12	13	14	15	16	17	18	19	20
RT (msec)	418	706	830	584	515	222	740	582	398	661
Age (yrs)	24.7	41.5	51.3	45.8	19.0	10.0	57.4	32.2	19.7	25.7

Subject No.	21	22	23	24	25	26	27	28	29	30
RT (msec)	605	890	717	610	803	702	241	360	890	424
Age (yrs)	52.1	55.4	46.0	38.6	39.7	34.4	15.0	29.2	59.5	32.0

6. Use the assigned software to demonstrate that Pearson r is independent of scaling factors.

Chapter 7

Chapter 7 of the textbook discusses the topic of regression. Statistical software can be a great help in doing the graphs and computations contained in this section.

1. If the assigned software allows, graph a scatter plot of the IQ and GPA data shown in Table 7.1 on p. 130 of the text and the least squares regression for these data. Compare your answer with Figure 7.3 on p. 134.
2. Using the data of Problem 13, p. 152 of the textbook:
   a. Use the assigned software to construct a scatter plot of the data with the least-squares regression line graphed on the plot. Put advertising costs on the X-axis and profits on the Y-axis.
   b. Describe the relationship shown in the graph.
   c. Use the assigned software to compute r and r^2.
   d. Use the assigned software to compute the least-squares regression line for predicting profits from advertising costs.
   e. Use the assigned software to compute the standard error of estimate.
   f. In August, the manager plans to spend $17,000 on advertising. Based on the least-squares regression line, how much profit should he expect that month (round to the nearest $1000)?

3 A psychology professor is interested in the relationship between grade point average (GPA) in graduate school and Graduate Record Exam (GRE) scores. A random sample of 20 graduate students is used for the study. The GPA and GRE score for each student is shown in the table that follows.
   a. Use Minitab to construct a scatter plot of the paired scores. Label the Y-axis variable "GPA" and the X-axis variable "GRE."
   b. Describe the relationship shown in the graph.
   c. Use Minitab to construct the least-squares regression line for predicting GPA from GRE scores.

d. Based on the regression line, what GPA would you predict for a student having a GRE score of 643?

Student No.	1	2	3	4	5	6	7	8	9	10
GPA	3.70	3.18	2.90	2.93	3.02	2.65	3.70	3.77	3.41	2.38
GRE	637	562	520	624	500	500	700	680	655	525

Student No.	11	12	13	14	15	16	17	18	19	20
GPA	3.54	3.12	3.21	3.35	2.60	3.25	3.48	2.74	2.90	3.28
GRE	593	656	592	689	550	536	629	541	588	619

4 Using the data of Figure 7.7 in the text on p. 146:

a. Use the assigned software to compute the multiple regression equation for predicting GPA from IQ and Study Time. Compare your equation with that given on p. 148 of the text.

b. Use the assigned software to compute R^2 for these data. Compare your answer with that given on p.150 of the text.

5. Use the assigned software to do Problem 16, p. 153 of the textbook.

6. A physician is interested in determining how accurately she can predict the weight of her patients by knowing their height and percent body fat. The height and percent body fat of a random sample of 14 female patients are measured. The following are the scores.

Patient No.	1	2	3	4	5	6	7	8	9	10	11	12	13	14
Weight (lbs)	105	113	117	120	124	126	127	128	130	135	138	141	150	155
Height (in)	61	65	63	70	68	64	60	62	70	68	66	72	67	73
Body fat (%)	20	17	19	15	23	23	26	27	28	24	33	35	37	38

a. Use the assigned software to do a scatter plot of weight and height. Use height as the X-axis variable.

b. Use the assigned software to compute Pearson r between weight and height.

c. How much of the variability in weight is accounted for by height?

d. Use the assigned software to derive the least-squares regression line for predicting weight given height.

e. Based on this regression line, what weight would you predict for subject 4? What is the error in this prediction?

f. Next, using the assigned software, derive the least-squares regression line for predicting weight given both height and percent body fat.

g. How much of the variability in weight is accounted for by these two variables taken together?

h. Based on the multiple regression line, what weight would you predict for subject 4? What is the error in prediction? Compare your answer with the answer to part **e**.

Chapter 13

Chapter 13 of the textbook discusses the t test for single samples. Using the computer makes computation of t_{obt} and the obtained probability very easy. Since the computer gives the obtained probability, it is not necessary to compare t_{obt} with t_{crit}. Instead, compare the obtained probability given by the computer with the alpha level and conclude following the decision rule

If the obtained probability $\leq \alpha$, reject H_0
If the obtained probability $> \alpha$, retain H_0

1. Use the assigned software to analyze the data given in Table 13.4 on p. 296 for the First Word Utterances illustrative problem. Remember for this problem, $\alpha = 0.05_{2\ tail}$. Compare your value of t_{obt} with that given on p. 296, and your conclusion with that given on p. 295.

2. Use the assigned software to do Practice Problem 13.1 on p. 297 of the textbook. Compare your answer with that given on p. 298.

3. Using the percentage of fat data of Problem 19 on p. 310 of the text.
   a. Employ the assigned software to test the directional H_1 of that problem. Use $\alpha = 05_{1\ tail}$.
   b. Although H_1 was retained in part a, the physician notes that the sample mean was in the right direction. She suspects that the failure to reject H_1 was due to running too few subjects (low power). Therefore she conducts the experiment again, this time using a random sample of 36 men from her corporation. The following percentages of fat were obtained: 26, 24, 31, 40, 31, 29, 30, 32, 35, 33, 23, 25, 17, 15, 20, 22, 20, 18, 23, 25, 18, 16, 25, 27, 22, 42, 27, 34, 31, 27, 13, 24, 16, 27, 14, 29. Using the new sample data and $\alpha = 05_{1\ tail}$, use the assigned software to test the directional H_1.
   c. Using the assigned software and the new sample data, construct the 95% confidence interval for the population mean.
   d. Using the assigned software and the new sample data, construct the 99% confidence interval for the population mean.

4. A student consumer-advocate group believes the amount of money students pay for college textbooks has risen dramatically in the current year. In the previous year, the mean expenditure per student was $215.25. A random sample of 30 students is taken from the group's college and the amount spent on textbooks by each student this year is recorded. The following data in dollars were obtained: 253, 220, 261, 205, 270, 200, 245, 225, 260, 210, 265, 205, 242, 228, 257, 213, 262, 208, 252, 218, 267, 203, 272, 198, 230, 240, 232, 242, 237, 233.
   a. Assume that the group is also interested in determining whether the amount spent this year has decreased. Using the assigned software, test the nondirectional H_1. Use $\alpha = 05_{2\ tail}$.
   b. Using the assigned software, construct the 95% confidence interval for the population mean.

Chapter 14

Chapter 14 of the textbook discusses the *t* test for correlated groups and the *t* test for independent groups. In the exercises that follow you will use the assigned software to analyze data using these tests.

1. Use the assigned software to solve Practice Problem 14.1 on p. 317 in the text. Compare your answer with that given in the practice problem.

2. Use the assigned software to solve Problem 14.2 on p. 319. Compare your answer with that given in the practice problem.

3. Use the assigned software to solve Problem 23 on p. 345. Compare your answer with that given in Appendix C.

4. Use the assigned software to analyze the data given in Table 14.5 on p. 328 of the text. Compare your analysis with that given on p. 329.

5. An educator is interested in determining if divorce affects school performance. A study is conducted comparing sixth-grade reading scores for a random sample of 30 children having married parents with those of a sample of 30 children having divorced parents. The following data are obtained. The higher the score, the better is the performance. One subject in the divorced group had to be dropped due to illness and was not replaced. Use $\alpha = 0.05_{2\text{ tail}}$, to evaluate the nondirectional H_1.

Divorced	75	97	60	70	57	93	85	47	57	65
Married	74	71	86	64	91	94	61	54	99	76

Divorced	96	90	78	95	72	60	81	55	69	98
Married	74	86	68	96	58	49	97	79	73	82

Divorced	84	77	66	73	87	87	63	67	90	
Married	68	85	67	87	64	91	61	93	83	79

6. A health psychologist wants to evaluate the effects of a particular diet on weight. Thirty-five obese male volunteers are randomly selected and put on the diet for 3 months. Baseline and end-of-program weights are recorded for each subject. The weights (in pounds) shown here are obtained:

Subject #	1	2	3	4	5	6	7	8	9	10	11	12
Baseline	210	213	190	220	235	265	258	198	271	195	241	212
End of Program	200	201	185	210	230	245	263	193	261	184	237	200

Subject #	13	14	15	16	17	18	19	20	21	22	23	24
Baseline	261	272	185	242	266	247	232	170	243	180	275	248
End of Program	246	252	167	231	251	241	227	155	240	185	262	223

Subject #	25	26	27	28	29	30	31	32	33	34	35
Baseline	261	269	278	210	252	258	249	214	182	246	271
End of Program	240	245	250	196	237	238	241	201	167	232	256

a. Use the assigned software and $\alpha = 0.05_{2\ \text{tail}}$ to evaluate the nondirectional H_1.
b. Analyze these data with the t test for independent groups. How do you explain the difference in outcome between part **a** and part **b**?

Chapter 15

Chapter 15 of the textbook discusses the one-way independent groups ANOVA. In the exercises that follow, you will practice using the assigned software to perform this analysis. You probably remember how laborious the calculations are for this test using a hand calculator. I think you will agree that its way easier using the assigned software.

1. Use the assigned software to do Practice Problem 15.1 on p. 361. Compare your analysis with that given in the practice problem.

2. The sets of numbers given in the table below were obtained from Table J, the table of random numbers, in Appendix D.

Group 1	Group 2	Group 3
8	7	0
2	5	7
7	6	0
5	3	2
2	1	6
6	7	2
	4	5
	1	

a. Use the assigned software to perform a one-way independent groups ANOVA with $\alpha = 0.05$ to determine if there is a significant difference among the groups.
b. Add a constant of 4 to each score in Group 2, and a constant of 8 to each score in Group 3. This process is analogous to what concerning the population scores? Compute, the analysis of variance again and explain any differences between this result and that of part **a**.

2. Use the assigned software to solve Problem 20 on p. 376. Compare your analysis with that given in Appendix C.

3. A computer manufacturer is interested in determining the effects of various screen colors on visual clarity. An experiment is conducted in which 60 subjects are randomly divided into four groups of 15 subjects each. All subjects are given an acuity test via the computer screen. Subjects in group I see white letters on a black background; subjects in group 2 see black letters on a white background; subjects in group 3 see white letters on a blue background; and subjects in group 4 see yellow letters on a black background. Each subject is instructed to adjust the letter and background intensity to the setting he or she would normally use if working at a computer for an extended period of time. The following visual acuity scores are obtained; the higher the score, the higher the visual acuity.

Group 1	Group 2	Group 3	Group 4
75	73	94	81
85	74	78	83
71	81	93	77
77	70	92	91
87	95	82	84
67	85	90	67
89	68	69	82
63	67	86	90
73	85	75	65
76	69	94	67
92	78	98	78
86	73	69	88
68	87	76	66
65	75	84	77
72	71	76	69

- Use the assigned software to do a one-way independent groups ANOVA on the data, with $\alpha = 0.05$ to evaluate the four screen presentation colors.

Chapter 17

Chapter 17 of the textbook discusses two-way independent groups ANOVA. In the exercises that follow, you will use the assigned software for this ANOVA analysis.

1. Use the assigned software to analyze the data given in the illustrative experiment involving the effect of exercise on sleep. These data are shown in Table 17.1 on p. 400 in the text.

2. The sets of numbers given below for each cell were obtained from the table of random numbers, Table J, in Appendix D.

	Factor B		
Factor A	Level 1	Level 2	Level 3
Level 1	7	5	2
	5	7	2
	6	3	7
	4	4	4
	6	6	5
Level 2	2	4	7
	6	9	8
	2	6	4
	8	0	5
	1	8	2

a. Use the assigned software and do a two-way independent groups ANOVA with $\alpha = 0.05$ to determine if there are any significant main or interaction effects.
b. Add a constant of 3 to each score in row 1(Level 1 row of Factor A in the above data table). This process is analogous to what concerning a main or interaction effect? Compute the two-way analysis of variance again, and explain any differences between this result and that of part **a**.
c. Using the original scores, add a constant of 3 to each score in column 2 (Level 2) and a constant of 6 to each score in column 3 (Level 3). This process is analogous to what concerning a main or interaction effect? Compute the two-way analysis of variance again, and explain any differences between this result and that of part **a**.
d. Using the original scores, add a constant of 3 to all the scores of cell 11 of the above data table. This process is analogous to what concerning a main or interaction effect? Compute the two-way analysis of variance again, and explain any differences between this result and that of part b.

3. Use the assigned software to solve problem 10 on p.416. Compare your answer with that given in Appendix C.

4. A researcher is interested in determining if the effects of marijuana vary with prior usage of the drug. An experiment is conducted in which 12 moderate users, 12 light users, and 12 students who have had no prior use of marijuana are randomly sampled from a college population. Within each usage level, half of the subjects are randomly assigned to a placebo condition and the other half to an experimental condition. In the placebo condition, each subject smokes two regular cigarettes that taste and smell like marijuana cigarettes. In the experimental condition, each subject smokes two marijuana cigarettes. Immediately after finishing their cigarettes, subjects are given a reaction time test. The following scores (in millisecs) are obtained.

Marijuana Usage	Placebo		Marijuana	
None	795	605	965	878
	700	752	865	916
	648	710	811	840
Light	800	610	843	665
	705	757	765	810
	645	712	713	776
Moderate	790	600	815	635
	695	752	735	782
	634	705	683	744

Use the assigned software to do a two-way independent groups ANOVA on the data, with $\alpha = 0.05$.

Chapter 18

Chapter 18 of the textbook discusses nonparametric inference tests. The most important test presented is chi-square. In the exercises that follow, you will use the assigned software to solve chi-square problems involving contingency tables.

1. Use the assigned software to analyze the data of the illustrative example dealing with political affiliation and attitude. These data are given in Table 18.2 on p. 424 of the text. Compare your answer with that given on p. 427 and 428.

2. A local beer company is doing some marketing research. The company wants to determine if there is a relationship between gender and preference for its light, dark, or regular beer. A random sample of 100 adult women and 100 adult men is taken from the beer drinking population living in the city where the company is located. Each individual is allowed to sample a small amount of each beer type and then is asked which one is preferred. The order in which the three types of beers are presented is counterbalanced over subjects. The following contingency table presents the resulting data. Entries are the number of men and women who preferred each type of beer.

	Beer Types			
	Light	Dark	Regular	
Men	25	35	40	100
Women	58	12	30	100
	83	47	70	200

   Is there a relationship between gender and preference for beer type? Use $\alpha = 0.01$.

3. Use the assigned software to solve Problem 23 on p. 452 of the textbook.

4. Use the assigned software to solve Problem 25 on p. 452 of the textbook.

http://psychology.wadsworth.com

The Wadsworth Group is the publisher of the following imprints:
Brooks/Cole, Duxbury, Heinle & Heinle, Schirmer, Wadsworth, and West.

WADSWORTH
THOMSON LEARNING

Visit Wadsworth online at **www.wadsworth.com**

For your lifelong learning needs: **www.thomsonlearning.com**

ISBN 0-534-57773-3

90000

9 780534 577735